NATIONAL GALLERY
WASHINGTON

Newsweek/GREAT MUSEUMS OF THE WORLD

NEW YORK, N.Y.

GREAT MUSEUMS OF THE WORLD

Editorial Director—Carlo Ludovico Ragghianti
Assistant—Giuliana Nannicini
Translation and Editing—Editors of ARTNEWS

NATIONAL GALLERY WASHINGTON

Texts by:
Giampaolo Gandolfo
Gian Lorenzo Mellini
Raffaele Monti
Anna Pallucchini
Licia Ragghianti Collobi
Pier Carlo Santini

Design:
Fiorenzo Giorgi

Published by

NEWSWEEK, INC.
& ARNOLDO MONDADORI EDITORE

1st Printing 1968
2nd Printing 1971
3rd Printing 1973
4th Printing 1974
5th Printing 1978

ISBN: Clothbound Edition 0-88225-232-1
ISBN: Deluxe Edition 0-88225-207-0

Library of Congress Catalog Card No. 68-20027

© 1968—Arnoldo Mondadori Editore—CEAM—Milan

© 1968—Photographs Copyright by Kodansha Ltd.—Tokyo

INTRODUCTION

JOHN WALKER, *Director*
National Gallery of Art, Washington, D.C.

The New World was a paradise for those seeking political liberty, economic opportunity or freedom of worship, but not for those involved in the practice of art. For as Renoir said: "It is at the museum that one learns to paint." And until the present century America was largely without museums. No models were available to imitate, no great works of art to establish criteria of excellence. It is not surprising that until George Bellows broke the tradition, every major American artist went abroad to study.

The American colonists did not disapprove of art, but they wanted their own art. They were eager patrons. They wished to have before themselves a visible reminder of what they were, as though by surrounding themselves with realistic paintings of themselves and their possessions, they could secure themselves against the enormity and the newness of the country in which they lived. As a result they developed a passion for portraiture. In 1829 John Neal, the first important American art critic, wrote: "You can hardly open the door of a best room anywhere without surprising, or being surprised by, the picture of somebody plastered to the wall and staring at you with both eyes and a bunch of flowers." But until the end of the nineteenth century, Americans had neither the means nor the time to develop significant collections of paintings from other periods and other cultures.

Without collections, however, American painters, with the exception of those artists who had an opportunity to study in Europe, remained provincial. The cure for this provincialism was to study, learn and thus understand the traditions of European painting. But to do this it was necessary that works of art by the greatest European masters be brought across the ocean. This began to happen around 1900. Museums were established in many of the principal cities on the Atlantic seaboard and as far west as Chicago. But despite the establishment in Washington in 1869 of the Corcoran Gallery, a privately endowed institution housing many major works of art, the nation's capital lagged behind at least a half dozen other cities.

The capital of the United States had to wait until 1941 before an adequate national gallery was opened to the public. That it should become one of the greatest art galleries in the world in a brief 27 years is a remarkable achievement. It was conceived, founded and endowed by Andrew W. Mellon, who served as Secretary of the Treasury in the administrations of Presidents Harding and Coolidge and who was ambassador to the Court of St. James's under President Hoover. The National Gallery is maintained by the Federal Government and is governed by a Board of Trustees consisting of the Chief Justice of the United States, the Secretary of State, the Secretary of the Treasury, the Secretary of the Smithsonian Institution and five private citizens.

According to David Finley, the first director of the Gallery, the thought of assembling in Washington an important collection of paintings and sculpture was discussed by Mr. Mellon as early as 1927, but it was not until 10 years later that a piece of land halfway between the Washington Monument and the Capitol was selected and ground for the new museum was broken. On it was constructed one of the largest marble buildings in the world. Mr. Mellon wished the new building erected in a style that would be timeless and that would harmonize with existing buildings in Washington. Classicism, the style which began in Greece, developed in Rome and was revived in the Renaissance, fulfilled these requisites.

The architect, John Russell Pope, had a flair for using classical orders to achieve dramatic effects. In this respect the National Gallery of Art is pre-eminent. The rose-tinted marble walls of the building are symmetrically broken by pilasters and niches. In the center of each main façade are monumental Ionic porticoes. These porticoes shelter the main entrances to the Gallery. Inside, the visitor enters a rotunda with a coffered dome upheld by towering columns of green-black marble. From the rotunda great halls designed for monumental sculpture lead to interior garden courts. These courts are filled with constantly changing arrangements of flowers from the Gallery's greenhouse. Branching out from the great halls and courts are the rooms for the permanent collections of paintings and sculpture.

Temporary exhibitions are held below the main floor, and, in addition, the collection of Chinese porcelains, French eighteenth-century furniture, rock crystals and the jewels bequeathed to the Gallery by Joseph and P. A. B. Widener are shown in one wing. Also on this floor are exhibition rooms for one of the world's greatest collections of small bronzes, medals and plaquettes given by the Samuel H. Kress Foundation, as well as the galleries and study rooms for the collection of graphic arts donated principally by Lessing J. Rosenwald.

The focus of the collection, however, is on painting and sculpture from the thirteenth to the present century, and these are shown on the main floor. Their installation is determined by a certain philosophy — a philosophy that assumes that a work of art is not to be looked upon primarily as a means of instruction but rather as a source of pleasure. It follows from this that it is more valuable to experience a work of art than it is to know its attribution, technique or sociological significance. Therefore, each painting and piece of sculpture is shown in a way that allows the visitor the maximum free and uninterrupted scrutiny. Ideally, one should see and experience only a single object of art at one time, but in a museum this is hardly possible. We have, however, spaced the paintings at double the usual interval, and we have paneled many rooms so that the style of the interior architecture provides, so to speak, a second frame.

The arrangement of the collection is chronological. By traversing the whole Gallery the visitor has an opportunity to see the development of Western painting and sculpture from Cimabue to Picasso. The selection of pictures reproduced in this volume offers the same opportunity.

One of the earliest paintings in the collection was probably executed in Constantinople in the thirteenth century. Such icons, "the artifice of eternity," show the formula that had been evolved during the first thousand years of Christian art. The austere Madonna and the statuesque Christ Child dwell in a world remote from ours. Theirs is the world of eternal values nobly described in the great writings of the Fathers of the Christian Church, which served as the intellectual background for paintings of this type.

St. Francis of Assisi, however, was already alive when this picture was painted, and his preachings were shortly to revolutionize art. The ardent religious feelings that were fanned to flame by the Franciscans with their new doctrine that nature is a mirror of divinity required a form of expression more human, more natural than the Byzantine *Enthroned Madonna and Child*.

Duccio, who was trained, perhaps, in Constantinople and therefore in the tradition of the *Enthroned Madonna and Child*, reveals this new spirit. He was the leading artist of Siena, of that exquisite town in central Italy once more powerful than Florence, and for centuries more creative than Rome. Duccio's panel, *The Calling of the Apostles Peter and Andrew*, originally came from an altarpiece, which hung above the high altar of the Cathedral of Siena. When the altarpiece was first placed in the Cathedral, it was considered so splendid that it was accompanied by a triumphal procession and a whole day was dedicated to prayers and to ceremonies in honor of the Virgin. In this panel there is a new delight in the events of everyday life which was brought into art by the spread of the teachings of St. Francis. The apostles holding the net heavy with fish, the squid and the crabs swimming in the sea, are all part of the new naturalism of the fourteenth century. But the figure of Christ still retains the severe majesty of Byzantine art. His robe is imperial blue, and a thin line of gold flickers along its edge to symbolize His royalty, His divinity and His remoteness.

Byzantine art became a formula; it was a noble formula that was modified, but on the whole accepted for all fourteenth-century Sienese pictures. In Florence, on the other hand, this formula was eventually rejected, though the process was gradual. In the splendid triptych attributed to Cimabue one still sees all the Byzantine conventions. The hands, for example, are rendered with four curved strokes to represent fingers, and a curved line in the opposite direction to represent a thumb. Contrast with this a *Madonna and Child* by Giotto, one of the greatest masterpieces in the National Gallery. In comparing these two pictures one realizes what Dante, who knew both painters, meant when he wrote, "Cimabue once held the field in painting, but today Giotto has the ascendancy."

Giotto was a revolutionary recognized by Florence for his genius. "One of the lights and glories of our city," wrote Boccaccio shortly after Giotto's death. "There was nothing in nature but he could imitate it with his pencil so well as to deceive our very senses making them to imagine that to be the very thing itself which was only his painting." The direction of Florentine painting for the next 200 years was indicated by Giotto's concentration on rendering objects as they are; flesh that is rounded, substantial, tangible; fingers that grasp real objects; forms as massive and solid as granite. Gone were the colorful, patterned surfaces of medieval painting. From then on, as Leonardo would write in the sixteenth century, the first object of the painter was "to make a flat plane appear as a body in relief and projecting from that plane."

Thus the early fourteenth-century *Madonna and Child* by Giotto records the Florentine departure from the Byzantine formula in the direction of three-dimensional form, and *The Calling of the Apostles Peter and Andrew* by Duccio reveals a second, Sienese departure from the Byzantine precedent in the direction of naturalism. Naturalism increased throughout the fourteenth century, and in the early decades of the fifteenth century it is to be found flowering in such enchanting paintings as *The Meeting of St. Anthony and St. Paul* by Sassetta and an assistant, with its bleached hills and its vibrant, dense foliage.

The same tendency toward naturalism is to be found in a painting by a Sienese contemporary of Sassetta, Giovanni di Paolo. On the left four rabbits play in a garden that is itself like a background in one of the *mille-fleurs* tapestries which were so popular in the fifteenth century. In this painting there is also a charming representation of St. Joseph warming his hands at a golden flame.

It is indeed tempting to linger among the fifteenth-century Sienese artists at the National Gallery, for there are many exquisite examples, but compared to the work of their contemporaries in Florence, Sienese art remained a backwater, a quiet, enchanted pool lying outside the mainstream of art.

In Florence the current of innovation, of novelty, swept onward. One of the greatest paintings in America is *The Adoration of the Magi* by Fra Angelico and Fra Filippo Lippi. Few works of art more clearly indicate the past and the future of painting. At first it may seem a conservative work with its rich patterns, its flowing lines and its flowerlike colors. In its spirit of devotion it is especially suggestive of the Middle Ages. But this noted painting also portends the future. The naked youths scrambling over the ruins to view the procession remain outside the sumptuous medieval scene. These pale refugees from classical statuary appear to be inserted into the painting as an exercise in human anatomy, an early example of the Renaissance obsession with the figure which was to culminate in the nudes of Michelangelo. Also the scene in the stable, where the horses of the devotees are being groomed and watered and their hooves checked for stones after the ride, is a foreshadowing of the everyday reality of later genre painting.

Landscape also begins to be handled in new and suggestive ways. In Domenico Veneziano's panel of St. John the Baptist putting aside his worldly rainment to don his hairshirt, the landscape for the first time comes out of the background and becomes a dynamic part of the composition. The gentle, modulated surfaces of the saint's figure appear particularly vulnerable against the hard planes and jagged thrusts of the mountain. The brittle, rarefied air of this upland plateau is dazzling in its clarity. The wilderness here represents more than a mere symbol. It produces a physical reaction in the viewer.

Renaissance humanism directed increasing attention to the individuality of each man. Men wanted to be immortalized. They wanted to be able to say to themselves: "So long as man can breathe, or eye can see, so long lives this, and this gives life to thee." Thus we find a series of magnificent portraits from the fifteenth century. Andrea del Castagno brilliantly analyzed the Renaissance intellectual, refined yet sensual: his suspicious, distrusting stare is that of a sitter intelligent enough to realize he is not being flattered. The Renaissance leader is summed up in another superb portrait, this time not of a Florentine but of a Venetian, in a penetrating characterization by Giovanni Bellini; one sees the typical Renaissance military leader, the *condottiere:* stern and ruthless, with the thin, uncompromising mouth of the authoritarian.

These two portraits tell more about the fifteenth century in Italy than many volumes of history. During the early sixteenth century there came over Italy a change that is brilliantly revealed in a portrait by Raphael of Bindo Altoviti, a Florentine banker. Here one senses a new softness and effeminacy, a new love of delicacy and grace that weakened the Italian states and left them unable to resist a devastating invasion from the North in the 1520s.

In these few illustrations of Italian painting we have noted how techniques in rendering masses and volumes, in landscape and in portraiture, each underwent a development. But there were two other problems that Florentine artists tried constantly to solve: first, how to add to the representation of three-dimensional form a suggestion of movement; and second, how to represent space in a way that would incorporate the newly evolved scientific principles of one-point perspective.

The Youthful David by Andrea del Castagno, painted around 1450, seizes and holds a moment of suspended action, the poised instant at the end of the pendulum's swing. The problem of how in a timeless medium to express a movement in time finds its solution here in the catching of that pause between action and reaction. David has just swung back his sling, his cloak sweeps forward, his body leans back, his left arm reaches out for balance; but included implicitly as well is the forward movement, the surge of the body, the swing of the sling, the release of the stone. The figure of David was painted on a leather shield which probably was carried in the processions preceding courtly jousts and tournaments.

Many of the greatest paintings in the National Gallery of Art were acquired by Mr. Mellon from the Soviet Union around 1930. Among them is *The Adoration of the Magi* by Botticelli, a painting that illustrates the interest of Florentine artists in perspective as well as their mastery in rendering motion. The spacing of the columns and supports in the monumental ruin, within which the Holy Family is placed, is carefully contrived to suggest how objects seen at a distance appear to diminish in size according to mathematical ratios. The pitched wooden roof which rests on the stone ruins of classical architecture symbolizes the birth of Christianity amid the remnants of the classical world. Beneath that roof all is calm. A serene Madonna contemplates her child; an ox and ass look sleepily on, a road winds off into the tranquil bluehilled countryside. But as the viewer's eye moves away from the peaceful center, movement grows in waves, as onlookers pray, converse, gesticulate, until on the right it reaches a climax in the rearing of the impatient horses which the grooms can barely restrain. Here the onlookers are actual portraits, the landscape perhaps the Cam-

11

pagna. Naturalism is joined to symbolism, and the whole is infused with a lyrical poetry.

From about 1480 through the first quarter of the sixteenth century, the treatment of landscape backgrounds in painting was developed and changed in many ways, always with an increasing sense of actuality. Perugino's *Crucifixion*, another great picture formerly in the Hermitage Gallery in Leningrad, is one of the noblest examples of landscape composition in existence. The view of sea stretching to the horizon fills us with the awe of endless space.

Perugino's way of composing space was passed on to his greatest pupil, Raphael, who further developed his master's technique of rendering a real but idealized world. The earliest of the five paintings by Raphael in the National Gallery is a small panel of *St. George and the Dragon*, painted about 1504–06. This may well be the most beautifully preserved panel by Raphael in existence. How enchantingly the landscape in the background conveys a sense of reality: we see a roadway passing under tall trees, and our eyes move to the hills and meadows and distant city basked in clear light.

In the famous *Alba Madonna* by Raphael, painted about six years later, there is an even more vivid sense of a particular place. The setting is very similar to the countryside in the upper Tiber valley, near Orvieto, a few score miles from Rome, a region which has changed very little in the last four hundred years.

With Raphael, landscape painting in central Italy reached a summit, but to the north, in Venice, artists were just beginning to treat nature in a new way that was to be of the very greatest significance in Western art. The *Adoration of the Shepherds* by Giorgione illustrates this extraordinary innovation. Light is conceived in a way different from Raphael's clarity. All the objects in Giorgione's scene melt into and become a part of an ambient atmosphere. Giorgione renders figures in such a way that they fuse with one another in the landscape until the whole scene attains a uniform atmospheric effect. The early morning clarity that marked the work of the Florentine masters changes here into the hazy sunlight of late afternoon.

The Feast of the Gods takes us a step further. As we now know from X-rays, Titian painted out part of the background originally executed by his master Giovanni Bellini, and substituted the mountain on the left for Bellini's simple, continuous grove of trees, thus transforming the original wooded landscape into a scene of majestic grandeur. Here, in a way never attempted by the Florentines, nature has become the dramatic protagonist.

With Jacopo Tintoretto, mood becomes still more important. Fitful bursts of light and wind-tossed waves create the setting for the apparition to the terror-stricken disciples of Christ walking calmly on the Sea of Galilee. But the ultimate in expressionistic landscape painting is not found in the work of Tintoretto, but in the canvases of his great pupil, El Greco. In the background of El Greco's treatment of the ancient legend of Laocoön, one sees a flickering vision of Toledo, the painter's adopted home, here substituted for ancient Troy, before whose walls the priest Laocoön and his sons were attacked by sea serpents to prevent their revealing the secret of the wooden horse, visible in the middle distance.

In many illustrations in this book you will be able to trace the evolution of Italian painting, particularly the full splendor of Venetian art as revealed in the works of Titian, Tintoretto and Veronese, and the great disseminator of their styles, El Greco, to its final afterglow in the lovely views of Guardi and Canaletto of the late eighteenth century.

Painting north of Italy can also be traced in the Gallery in the same chronological way. The founder of the fifteenth-century Flemish school and the leading artist of the North was Jan van Eyck, traditionally considered the discoverer of oil painting. Whether or not he discovered oil painting may be debated, but certainly he was the first to realize a naturalistic rendering of interior space or, in less technical terms, the effect of looking into a room through an open window or door. *The Annunciation*, another painting bought from the Soviet Union, illustrates van Eyck's most salient characteristics: his masterful suggestion of atmosphere through subtle gradations of light and his unequaled skill in rendering detail. Such was van Eyck's facility that the half-visible frescoes on the dimly lit walls of the church are painted with an impalpable delicacy, the jewels on the angel's robe are depicted with a hard microscopic precision.

With the new oil technique artists could paint out-of-door scenes like *The Rest on the Flight into Egypt* by Gerard David, where the whole landscape seems permeated with that misty blue light so characteristic of Flanders, David's homeland. The artist probably could have observed a scene like this many times, for the Holy Family is depicted as ordinary, fifteenth-century pilgrims at rest, the father knocking down nuts from a tree to feed his wife and baby. But as often happens in Flemish paintings, there is a symbolic meaning combined with this glimpse of daily life. The grapes the Christ Child is eating symbolize the Eucharist and His future suffering.

12 Flemish artists of the fifteenth century were equally skillful as portraitists. They created one of the most

entrancing types of female portraiture in the history of painting. Rogier van der Weyden's portrait is perhaps of Marie de Valengin, the natural daughter of Philip the Good of Burgundy. Particularly fascinating is the contrast between her high, intellectual forehead and her sensual mouth. It is as though the antipodes of human character met and were resolved in her enigmatic personality.

From Flanders the style of van Eyck and van der Weyden and other Flemish artists spread to Germany. The four great masters of German painting are all represented in the Gallery's collection. In *The Small Crucifixion* by Mathis Grünewald, a brutal naturalism destroys the pious euphemisms of Christianity. Christ hangs down from the cross, the torso's weight stretching the arms, the fingers gnarled as the body stiffens in death. The mouth gapes. The lips are blue, the belly distended, green and bloated. The crown of thorns is an emblem that draws blood. The preternatural light of the eclipsed sun throws the figures into lurid relief against the blackened sky and heightens the emotional effect of the physical agony of grief and suffering. Here, the actuality of death has overwhelmed the mystery of the crucifixion.

In contrast to the Grünewald, Albrecht Dürer's *Madonna and Child* attempts through the close imitation of Italian art to set standards for absolute beauty. But even though this painting reflects the study of monumental Italian art, and, in particular, of Bellini's Venetian prototypes, the influence of the North is readily apparent — for example, in the view from the window, with the *schloss* on the slope and the distant blue mountains, or in the escutcheons in the foreground, one of which has been identified as that of the Haller family from Nuremberg, Dürer's home town. Dürer was also a magnificent portrait painter. His incisive characterization of an unidentified priest, dated 1516 in the upper right hand corner, reflects the temper of the age that a year later at Wittenberg gave birth to the Reformation. The jutting chin is firm and resolute. The lips are tightly drawn into a thin, ascetic line and the asymmetrical eyes stare fixedly out, almost fanatically.

More charming are the portraits of the children by Lucas Cranach, the Elder and Hans Holbein the Younger. Holbein's portrait of Edward VI dowers a child of two with the essence of rank. The baby's face looks out from its royal robes with the withdrawn aloofness of majesty. One hand grasps a rattle as if a sceptre. The other is raised in a gesture of royal largess. While the Cranach portraits seem to be of children masquerading as princes and princesses, the Holbein becomes the portrait of a monarch masquerading as a child.

In the seventeenth century, the leadership in European painting was divided between three schools: Flanders, Holland and Spain. Many of the greatest masterpieces at the National Gallery are from this period. Van Dyck's portrait of the Marchesa Elena Grimaldi was painted in Genoa when the young artist was on the threshold of his brilliant career. His likeness of Philip, Lord Wharton was executed some ten years later, in England, where van Dyck had established himself as the leading portrait painter. In painting the Marchesa Grimaldi van Dyck reveals, as he does in many of his Genoese portraits, a formality indicative of a certain awe on the part of the painter toward his sitter; in this portrait the Marchesa dwells in a world apart from the artist. This attitude changes in van Dyck's English portraits where painter and sitter exist on more familiar terms. Yet in both paintings van Dyck brilliantly embodies the European conception of the great lady and the great gentleman.

Such aristocratic portraiture in the Grand Manner contrasts sharply with the bourgeois art of Holland. The three greatest Dutch artists were Rembrandt, Frans Hals and Vermeer. The National Gallery has *The Mill* by Rembrandt, a supreme achievement in landscape painting. John Constable, the great English landscapist, judged it "sufficient to form an epoch in art . . . the first picture in which a sentiment has been expressed by chiaroscuro only, all details being excluded." The hushed melancholy mood of the painting intimates the mortality of the domestic life going on in the foreground, unattending, as, in the gathering dusk, day fades into night. But Rembrandt's greatest fame was as a portraitist. His self-portrait shows the artist as he looked toward the end of his life, when time and misfortune had left their marks in the deep lines of his face. Rembrandt's eyes searched more profoundly into the human soul than those of any other artist, and here he seems weary with knowledge.

By comparison, his great contemporary, Frans Hals, appears somewhat superficial. Hals's sitters are easily pigeonholed in broad and obvious categories, but he will always appeal to those who appreciate the sheer virtuosity of his brushwork, who enjoy the rapid, volatile touch which builds up images with a few brilliant strokes.

The third of the great Dutch masters was Vermeer. In place of the dashing, impressionistic brushwork of Hals we find in his paintings a meticulous and careful approach. Whereas with Hals the sitter is seen in a quick glance, with Vermeer he is seen with a steady gaze. One is all nervous fire, the other liquid calmness. These two artists represent the extremes of the Dutch rendering of form.

Perfect balance between the two methods was achieved, not by a Dutch artist but by a Spaniard. In Velaz-   13 quez's study for the portrait of Pope Innocent X, there is a beauty of pigment and handling of the brush unsurpassed by Hals, but there is also an insight into character far beyond the power of any Dutch artist, except Rembrandt. But even Rembrandt distorts personality more than Velazquez. Where Rembrandt imbues his sitters with one mood — his own profoundly tragic attitude toward life — Velazquez shows them as they are, with an absolute detachment, leaving them with all the rich, complex variety which human nature affords. That is perhaps why one can return again and again to the great paintings by Velazquez without ever completely absorbing their full meaning.

After these titans among painters, the artists of the eighteenth century belong to a humbler, though gayer race. At the end of the eighteenth century, Spain produced one last painter of genius, Goya. The portrait of the Marquesa de Pontejos shows with what sly, malicious wit he portrayed the aristocracy of his day. Goya treats this insipid marquesa quite frankly as a fashion plate, and uses the occasion of her portrait to display his virtuosity. Particularly brilliant is the handling of the chiffon of her skirt, which obviously interested Goya much more than his sitter's vacuous expression.

But Goya was also a great master of characterization, a great novelist if you wish. He analyzed a domestic tragedy as brilliantly as it might have been by Dickens or Thackeray, among European writers, or by Lady Murasaki among Japanese. He portrayed his friend Sureda as a gay, charming companion, a fellow artist who enjoyed his wine and probably his women. But when he came home late at night with his friend, Goya, they saw Mrs. Sureda as the master depicted her, with her stiff little back, tight black curls, in an icy and unforgiving fury. No wonder Goya was something of a misogynist.

By underscoring the conflict between the social role and the personal character of his sitter, Goya introduced into portraiture a curious blend of sociological statement and psychological insight, new to art. Velazquez, for example, remains detached from his sitters, painting them as he finds them, not forcing the viewer to any conclusion. On the other hand, the subjects of Rembrandt are most convincing when they most aptly reflect his own tragic sense of life; and those of Franz Hals, while delightful, seem acquaintances not friends.

English portraits are never so penetrating. *The Frankland Sisters* by Hoppner is a good example. We have a description of Hoppner's working method, a procedure typical of eighteenth-century English portraitists, written by another painter, Northcote. "Hoppner frequently remarked," Northcote said, "that in painting ladies' portraits he used to make as beautiful a face as he could . . . working down from this beautiful state until the bystander should cry out, 'Oh, I see a likeness coming!' Whereupon he stopped and never ventured to make it more like."

The real contribution of English eighteenth-century painting, however, was in the field of landscape. Such scenes as Thomas Gainsborough's *Landscape with a Bridge* are purely imaginary, and it is said that Gainsborough conceived them sitting at a table covered with lumps of coal and bits of moss, which he observed under different illuminations. The originality of his interpretation of nature had little appeal to collectors, and at Gainsborough's death his house was filled with unsold landscapes.

John Constable, the greatest genius of English painting, also had a hard time making a living. One of his first important commissions was a view of Wivenhoe Park. When working on this landscape, Constable wrote that he had not got "so much in as they [the owners of the estate] wanted . . . But today I got over the difficulty and begin to like it myself." The owner's desire for as much of his property as possible to appear in the picture explains the unusually wide angle of the artist's view.

Another great English landscape painter was Turner. His work is magnificently represented in the Gallery by *Mortlake Terrace*, one of the most beautiful, as well as one of the most interesting of all his pictures. The Thames is depicted with boats and barges drifting down river in the misty light of late afternoon. One afternoon at the Royal Academy, while Turner was out to lunch, Landseer, the famous painter of dogs, decided Turner's landscape needed an accent in the center, so he cut out of paper a little dog and stuck it on the parapet. Turner was delighted, and the paper dog has remained there ever since.

The eighteenth-century American school was strongly influenced by British painting. Our three leading early artists — West, Copley and Stuart — spent much of their time in England. Benjamin West, the first of the expatriates, succeeded Sir Joshua Reynolds as President of the Royal Academy, and during the first decades of the eighteenth century was recognized as the foremost historical painter in England. He also did portraits, notably one of Colonel Guy Johnson with an Indian who may be Johnson's secretary and devoted friend, Joseph Brant.

West's studio was a haven for American painters working in England. Among those who received his advice and help, probably the most distinguished was John Singleton Copley, who left Boston in 1774 and settled permanently in England. Copley's famous group portrait shows himself and his family shortly after their arrival in London. The artist is the figure standing on the left looking over his right shoulder.

Another who received West's help was Gilbert Stuart. The characterization, the design, and the color in his portrait of *Mrs. Richard Yates* make this one of the greatest of all American portraits, superior in some ways to anything done at the same time in England.

Among American artists of the nineteenth century, two of our greatest painters went to France. Whistler painted *The White Girl*, a portrait of his model and mistress, Jo, in 1862 and sent it to the Salon the next year. It was refused and consequently had the greater distinction of being shown with the Impressionists at the Salon des Refusés.

Mary Cassatt, like Whistler, joined the Impressionists and spent most of her life in Paris. *Girl Arranging Her Hair* was painted as a challenge to Degas, who said no woman had a sense of style. In this picture Miss Cassatt has taken the pose of Michelangelo's *Bound Slave* in the Louvre and adapted it to a scene of modern life.

For three centuries, French painting has been the most creative school in Western art. The National Gallery contains works of the great masters of seventeenth-century Classicism: Poussin and Claude; of naturalism: Le Nain and later Chardin; and of that specifically French eighteenth-century style which, for lack of a better name, we call the Rococo: Watteau, Boucher, Fragonard. French nineteenth-century Neo-Classicism and Realism are well represented by major works of J. L. David and Ingres, as are the subsequent revolutionary movements in French painting: Romanticism led by Géricault and Delacroix; Realism by Courbet; Impressionism by Manet, Monet, Pissarro and others; and Post-Impressionism marked by the work of such towering geniuses as Cézanne, Gauguin and van Gogh.

Many paintings by these artists are illustrated, but there are two pictures, both of children, I would like to mention specifically. The first is a portrait of a child with her nurse by Manet. The charm of the painting may make one forget that this canvas embodies a revolutionary approach to art — Impressionism. The composition has the informality and the immediacy characteristic of the new movement. The Impressionist painter, instead of inventing his composition out of his imagination, watched the kaleidescope of appearance until he found in this moving pattern an arrangement suggesting a significant design. This fortuitous, ready-made composition he would hold in his memory as the basis for some subsequent picture. Manet glimpsed a woman and a child against the verticals of an iron railing and snapped the scene mentally, much as it might have been snapped photographically, but at the same time he gave his picture a timeless quality far beyond the power of the camera. This canvas is believed to be the first picture of considerable size painted mostly out of doors by the artist.

Another bewitching painting of a child, in this case by Renoir, illustrates another aspect of Impressionism: the extraordinary technical innovations introduced by these French painters. Here the scene on the canvas is woven, so to speak, out of a web of brilliantly colored brushstrokes that, from a distance, fuse in the retina of the eye to form the image of a child standing on a garden path surrounded with flowers. Because the same threads of color, varied only in intensity, are used throughout the picture, the little girl seems a part of a single, permeating substance of which flesh and earth, clothes and flowers, are different aspects. It is not surprising that Renoir's canvas is one of the most popular pictures in the National Gallery of Art. The Gallery's Permanent Collection is limited to the work of artists who have been dead for at least twenty years. But another part of the collection contains the work of artists still alive or more recently deceased. The representation of Picasso, Braque, Modigliani, Matisse, Derain and other members of the Paris school is among the best in the world.

The reproductions in this book are, necessarily, only colored shadows of the actual paintings in the collection of the National Gallery of Art, but I hope they will give the reader some sense of the exalted pleasure he will feel if he has the opportunity to see the originals. We have had many visitors. We hope we may have many more, for the National Gallery of Art belongs not only to the people of the United States, but to the people of the whole world. We want you to feel with us a pride in its existence, to look upon it as a reservoir of human creativity where you can share in the achievements of many of the greatest geniuses of the world of art.

ITALY

DUCCIO DI BUONINSEGNA. *The Calling of the Apostles Peter and Andrew*

This exquisite small picture is the third or fourth predella panel from the back of Duccio's great double-sided altarpiece, the *Maestà*, commissioned in October 1308 by Giacomo Mariscotti, who stipulated that the artist devote himself entirely to this project and complete it before taking on any other work. A reconstruction of Duccio's career leads one to suppose he was born about 1255; in 1308 he was therefore at the height of his powers. This complex work, which included the Madonna with saints and angels on the large central panel and an undetermined number of secondary panels depicting scenes from the life of Christ, was immediately appreciated as something extraordinary by Duccio's fellow Sienese. Upon its completion in June 1311, it was carried to the cathedral in solemn procession, accompanied by "trumpets, clarionets and castanets." Succeeding generations did not show the same respect; in 1771 the double-sided altarpiece was sawn in half and several elements were cut out from it.

As a mature work, the *Maestà* shows Duccio's particular genius for assimilating the diverse cultural cross-currents to which he could have been exposed not only in Siena, but also in Florence, and especially in Pisa where the persistence of a Hellenizing tradition contributed to the revival of sculpture under the Pisani and Arnolfo di Cambio.

We can easily measure Duccio's eclecticism as well as his own originality by recalling that the *Maestà* is almost contemporary with Giotto's Arena Chapel. Even though recent research has revealed many other components in his style, Duccio's exalted spirituality is based on Byzantine art, not archaic Byzantine stereotypes, but the rethought models of the Paleologue cultural revival. Nor can one overlook the echoes of the precious maniaturist tradition, then flowering in Northern Europe and, by its nature, easily transportable far afield.

Even this small portion of his masterpiece reveals the fundamental gifts of the great Sienese. His lack of concern for illusionistic spatial effects is evident: the rocky spur on the left is simply a theatrical backdrop, only the horizontal placement of the boat divides the remaining space into zones; nor can we speak of naturalism in describing the elusively green sea where the apostles' net is full of weightless fish. But Christ's beckoning gesture expresses a power that seems to threaten the boat's fragile balance and to arouse an inward transformation in the humble fishermen.

The exquisite cadence of gestures, the subtle and restrained treatment of forms in relief and the luminous color which seems to model material like malleable wax are all elements of Duccio's poetic vision.

GIOTTO. *Madonna and Child*   *p. 20*

This painting is evidently the center of a polyptych whose other elements have been identified on stylistic grounds as *St. Stephen* in the Horne Museum, Florence, *St. Lawrence* and *St. John the Baptist* in the Musée André, Châalis. The fifth panel is lost.

The polyptych has been variously connected with that noted by Ghiberti

DUCCIO DI BUONINSEGNA
Siena, active from 1278 to 1319
The Calling of the Apostles Peter and Andrew
(circa 1308–1311)
Panel; 17 1/8″ × 18 1/8″.
With eight or nine other panels, this was once part of the predella on the rear of the double-sided altar, called the *Maestà*, painted between 1308 and 1311 for the Siena cathedral, commissioned by Giacomo Mariscotti.
Samuel H. Kress Collection, 1939.

GIOTTO
Florence 1266(?) — Florence 1336
Madonna and Child (1320–1330)
Panel; 33 5/8″ × 24 3/8″.
Samuel H. Kress Collection, 1939.

and Vasari in the Badia, Florence, or with one of the four cited by Ghiberti as being in Sante Croce, in this instance in the Peruzzi Chapel. None of these identifications has been universally accepted, but scholars do agree on a 1320–1330 dating because the picture reflects Giotto's style seen in the Peruzzi and Bardi Chapels, allowing, of course, for the inherent differences in work composed for ample chapel walls and that constricted to the space of compartments in a polyptych.

After Giotto's dramatic triumphs in Assisi and Padua, "in the manner of the great medieval romances," the Florentine frescoes open a third chapter in his career. The Santa Croce frescoes record the artist's aspiration towards a harmony and equilibrium at once anticipatory of, but at the same time parallel to, the Humanist culture developing between Florence and Padua where he evolved his style in the first quarter of the century. Giotto's fusion of intellect and sentiment is expressed in his search for a solemn and continuous space as well as in the breadth of his modeling which conveys a sense of plastic form together with the inward motivation of action. His simplified compositions, functional line and vibrating luminosity underline the beauty of emotive details.

Such are the qualities of the splendid *Madonna* reproduced here. It is enough to compare this painting with the Uffizi's austere *Virgin* of about 1310, whose weight bears so heavily on the fragile throne, to see how far Giotto had evolved. The outlines of the Madonna, seen here in a three-quarter view, create a sinuous and elegant line whose musical lyricism is interrupted by the almost geometric block of the Child. Against the gold ground and the green drapery which gently enfolds her, the Madonna's flesh glows luminously with subtle passages of transition. Without at all denying his own most personal qualities, Giotto seems closer in this picture than in any other of his works to the poetry of his great contemporary in Siena, Simone Martini.

GIOVANNI DI PAOLO. *The Expulsion from Eden*

The predella panel from which this detail is reproduced belongs to the artist's middle period, later than his formative Sienese phase when he admired Ambrogio Lorenzetti's perspective innovations and the new narrative style of Gentile da Fabriano and Sassetta. These were the sources of Giovanni di Paolo's taste for the fantastic and the fabulous.

A bizarre angel, whose sharp wings flutter like a beetle's and whose curls are whipped back from the violence of flight, is thrusting Adam and Eve from the symbolic threshold of Paradise. Adam is naked and docile; Eve maintains her dignity with fragile grace. The modeling of their bodies is especially refined. The exiles' new Eden, full of innocent, happy animals and of plants laden with flowers and fruit, is like those wondrous *mille-fleures* tapestries of the 15th century. Giovanni di Paolo's taste was not unlike Henri Rousseau's who also composed fantastic forests from the vocabulary of everyday nature (see p. 95).

GIOVANNI DI PAOLO
Siena 1403 — Siena 1482
The Expulsion from the Garden of Eden.
Detail from *The Annunciation* (1440–1450)
Panel; 15 3/4″ × 17 3/4″.
One panel from a predella that included the *Nativity,* Vatican Gallery; *Crucifixion,* Dahlem Museum, Berlin; *The Presentation in the Temple,* Metropolitan Museum, New York; and *The Adoration of the Magi,* Cleveland Museum of Art.
Samuel H. Kress Collection, 1939.   **21**

SASSETTA. *The Meeting of St. Anthony and St. Paul — St. Anthony Distributing His Wealth to the Poor*

These enchanting scenes from the life of St. Anthony have provoked a flood of literature and arguments over the attribution to Sassetta. The intervention of assistants, as modestly talented as Vico di Luca or as gifted as Sano di Pietro, would explain the varying levels of quality and still enable one to attribute to Sassetta the over-all concept of the series as well as such fine panels as the *Meeting*. The *Meeting* demonstrates the narrative skill found in documented Sassetta, like the *Madonna of the Snows* predella or the Borgo San Sepolcro altar. Like Giovanni di Paolo, Sassetta was aware of the advances the Florentine School had made in representing the world rationally, but he preferred the Sienese courtly tradition that inclined to an archaizing style.

This panel, following an old convention, presents three scenes in one: Anthony sets out at the upper-left to find his companion; he blesses the centaur, symbol of the pagan world; and finally meets with Paul outside the cave. All this takes place in a landscape dense with woods, under a horizon high above the airy hills. Instead of sky there is an abstract gold ground that seems to emphasize the preciousness with which objects and events are treated. A masterful touch is the repetition of the linear theme

SASSETTA
Cortona — active in Siena from 1423 to 1450, the year of his death
The Meeting of St. Anthony and St. Paul
St. Anthony Distributing His Wealth to the Poor
(circa 1440)
Panels; each 18 3/4″ × 13 5/8″.
These and two other panels in the National Gallery, two in the Yale University Art Gallery, one in the Robert Lehman Collection, New York, and one in the Dahlem Museum, Berlin, almost certainly accompanied a large central figure of St. Anthony Abbot.
Samuel H. Kress Collection, 1939, 1952.

created by the hill, the cave and the two saints posed in a tender yet solemn embrace.

On the other hand, the greater naturalism of *St. Anthony Distributing His Wealth to the Poor* is reminiscent of the example set by Gentile da Fabriano and suggests, particularly in the detailed grandiose setting, the intervention of Sano di Pietro.

FRA ANGELICO
Vicchio circa 1400 — Rome 1455
FILIPPO LIPPI
Florence circa 1405 — Spoleto 1469
The Adoration of the Magi (circa 1445)
Panel; diameter 54".
Samuel H. Kress Collection, 1952.

FRA ANGELICO AND FRA FILIPPO LIPPI.   *The Adoration of the Magi*
This picture is justly famous for its high formal qualities, for its enchanting subject matter and, finally, for the difficulty in precisely identifying who conceived and executed the work. The tondo had been generally identified

with the one by Fra Angelico cited in the 1492 Medici inventory made at the death of Lorenzo the Magnificent and appraised for 100 *fiorini,* an extremely high value.

But 19th-century critics quite properly pointed out elements of Filippo Lippi's style in the painting and were on the point of attributing the entire work to him, under the influence of Fra Angelico. However recent criticism has accepted the more measured and convincing solution that the work is the fruit of a collaboration between the two masters, each of whose contributions can be distinguished, but who were able, through a certain spiritual affinity, to co-operate in creating a masterpiece.

Fra Angelico is thought to have conceived the work, employing a traditional International Gothic motif, to have executed the central group of the Madonna and Child and to have generally endowed the work with its spring-like and joyful orchestration of color. His departure for Rome in 1445 would account for his leaving the composition unfinished. Lippi's part was to provide the happy incidents of the story, the brilliant narrative invention, the landscape and those vivacious passages that enliven the bustling animate and inanimate world. The prediliction for massive architectural arrangements as well as recurring genre motifs indicate his awareness of Northern art. The early date of this extraordinary collaboration, about 1445, accounts for the paramount influence of Fra Angelico's style in the work. By that time Filippo Lippi had not yet evolved his own individual style where line was used not for its decorative qualities but strictly to define form.

FRANCO–FLEMISH SCHOOL (?)   *Profile Portrait of a Lady*
Until 1921 this extremely beautiful portrait of a courtly lady was unanimously attributed to Pisanello. Richter was the first to propose an entirely different origin for the painting and his opinion that it is a work of the Franco-Flemish School has been as enthusiastically endorsed by scholars as had been the earlier attribution to Pisanello. This is not as strange as it may seem, for the painting is clearly a product of that refined Late Gothic style that spread through all of Europe. This style was particularly popular in northern Italy where in fact Pisanello, Tuscan by origin but trained in Verona, did most of his work.

The lady depicted here has a somewhat Northern profile, and her sumptuous blue dress embroidered in gold and her complicated and refined hairdo both recall the fashions of the Burgundian court. Of particular interest is the artist's extraordinary sense of stylization. The irregular profile is like a playful Gothic line; the drawing of the shell-like ear is a decorative whim as is the headdress and the coiffure.

FRANCO–FLEMISH SCHOOL (?)
Beginning of the 15th Century
Profile Portrait of a Lady
Panel; 20 3/8″ × 14 3/8″.
Andrew Mellon Collection, 1937.

24

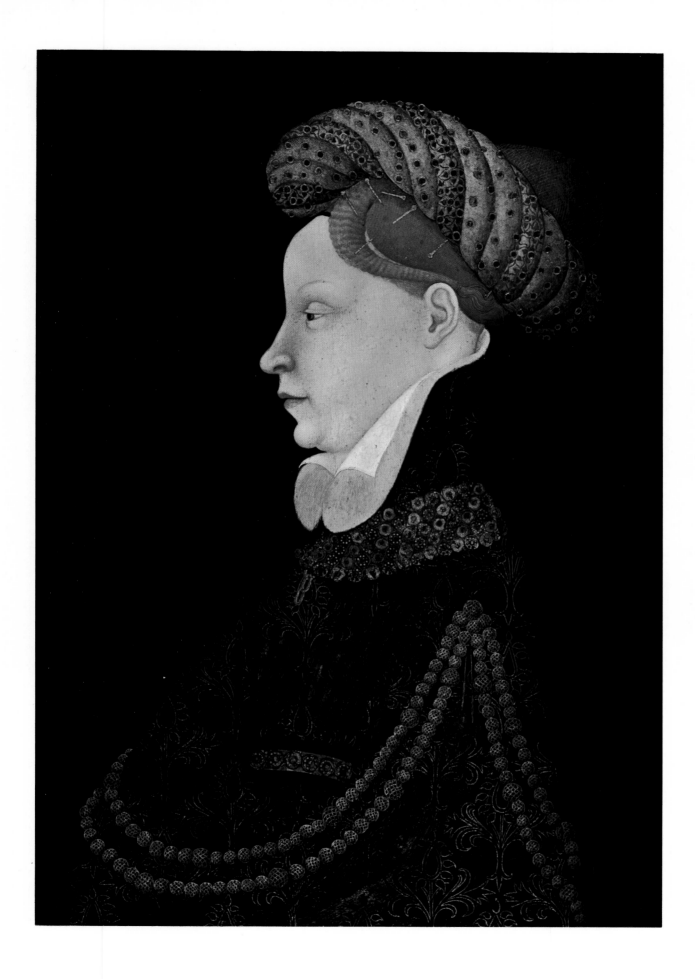

DOMENICO VENEZIANO. *St. John in the Desert*

Domenico Veneziano is now recognized as one of the most important figures of the Early Renaissance in Florence, but so few of his works have
survived, it is difficult to reconstruct his career. His pre-Florentine origins
may have been connected with Venice and Verona. Gentile Bellini, Maso-
lino and Jacopo Bellini may have made him aware of problems of light.

There is no doubt that this painting is from his hand and dates between 1445
and 1448, soon after Domenico's St. Egidius cycle. The theme is rather
unusual, St. John putting aside his clothes as he enters the desert, and certainly is to be understood as symbolizing the renunciation of worldly van-
ities.

The beautiful drawing of the nude has passages of a Praxitelean subtlety.

DOMENICO VENEZIANO
Venice (?) circa 1400 — Florence 1461
St. John in the Desert (circa 1445)
Panel; 11 1/8″ × 12 3/4″.
This panel, *St. Francis Receiving the Stig-
mata,* also in the National Gallery of Art,
The Annunciation and *The Miracle of St.
Zenobius,* both in the Fitzwilliam Museum,
Cambridge, and *The Martyrdom of St. Lucy*
in the Dahlem Museum, Berlin, formed
the predella of the altarpiece executed for
the church of S. Lucia dei Magnoli, Flor-
ence, and now in the Uffizi.
Samuel H. Kress Collection, 1943.

The young athlete dominates the imaginary mountain landscape whose forms, though softened, evoke Gothic art. Blue sky has replaced the gold ground, and masses find their proper location in this new airiness. Above all, the artist used light to create a space whose silent solemnity underlines the decisive act of the saint.

ANDREA DEL CASTAGNO.   *Portrait of a Man*
If formal coherence is a measure of artistic worth, then this portrait is a model of excellence. The sitter occupies almost all the space of the panel, but more importantly he seems to overcome the imaginary space with his disdainful expression and grim look. Light and shadow combine to emphasize the plasticity of his form. His curls have an almost geometrical regu-

27

larity, and the folds of the drapery, gathered in a splendidly drawn hand expressive of suppressed internal violence, give an implacable solidity to the figure. This portrait is considered close in style to the solemn figures in the *Last Supper* in St. Apollonia (1455–1450), Florence, but was probably painted slightly earlier, for the luminous drawing of the face and hand indicate that the artist was not yet far removed from the influences of Domenico Veneziano and Piero della Francesca as is indicated in his frescoes for the Chapel of St. Egidius (1439).

SANDRO BOTTICELLI. *Portrait of a Youth*
It is strange that it has only been since Berenson's 1922 attribution that this picture has been firmly associated with Botticelli, particularly curious in view of the high quality of the picture and its typical Botticelli features. The young man in a brown coat and with a red hat holding back his blond

SANDRO BOTTICELLI
Florence 1445 — Florence 1510
Portrait of a Youth (circa 1487)
Panel; 16 1/4″ × 12 1/2″.
Andrew Mellon Collection, 1937.

28

hair is a thoughtful characterization and full of aristocratic reserve. The hand seems to be placed on the chest not in any significant gesture, but to display its perfect anatomy. His connection with the young ephebus in the *Madonna of the Pomegranates* suggests a date about 1487.

SANDRO BOTTICELLI. *The Adoration of the Magi*

This is one of Botticelli's favorite and frequently treated themes. The closest precedent, also in time, is certainly the Uffizi picture of 1475–1478 with its analogous emphasis on the actuality of the events, here witnessed by a crowd of contemporary Renaissance figures. But in the Uffizi picture space is conceived entirely differently; people gather more naturalistically to peer curiously at the Holy Family camped between a broken wall and an inhospitable rock. By contrast, in this treatment the Adoration is divided physically and psychologically into two groups masterfully disposed in a

SANDRO BOTTICELLI
The Adoration of the Magi
(circa 1481–1482)
Panel; 27 5/8" × 41".
Andrew Mellon Collection, 1937.

29

SANDRO BOTTICELLI
Giuliano de' Medici (circa 1478)
Panel; 29 3/4" × 20 5/8".
Samuel H. Kress Collection, 1952.

stepped arrangement within a strictly limited space. The sinuous line of single figures is arranged with the utmost skill while the central motif, the ruins of a classical temple, dominates the composition and contributes to its harmony. The direction of adoring groups enhances the deep recession into a green and mountainous landscape, a complete novelty in Botticelli's work. Even if the picture were not mentioned in old documents, this passage alone would be sufficient to date the painting to the beginning of Botticelli's Roman period (1481–1482).

SANDRO BOTTICELLI. *Giuliano de' Medici*

Critics have puzzled over the autograph qualities and chronological order of four versions of Giuliano's portrait. This one is undoubtedly the most complete and authoritative likeness. The half-open door and the turtle-

dove, allusions to death and mourning, lead one to think that the painting must have been executed immediately after Giuliano's assassination.

This would seem to be Botticelli's melancholy tribute to a lost friend. An immobile, marmoreal face detaches itself from a rarefied atmosphere. Against a gloomy ground a black mass of hair contrasts with the cold blue sky. The geometric precision of the architectural setting is like an abstract game and anticipates Bronzino's frosty conceptions.

PIETRO PERUGINO.   *The Crucifixion*

The painting is also known as the Galitzin Triptych, after the Russian princely collection to which it belonged until passing into the Hermitage in 1886. (It was bought by Andrew Mellon from the U.S.S.R. in 1931.) In the past the painting's high qualities led critics to assign it to Raphael,

but it is now universally accepted as the masterpiece of Perugino's early maturity, while he was working in the Sistine Chapel (1481) or immediately thereafter.

Although the painting is subdivided into three panels, a continuous landscape welds the composition into a whole. Rocky outcroppings on each side, reminiscent of Perugino's youthful *St. Bernard* in Perugia, lead the eye into the far distance where sea and sky melt into one. The painting might be better called a meditation on the death of Christ, such is the expression of those depicted: St. Jerome, the Virgin, St. John and Mary Magdalen.

Space is deftly created by means of linear perspective and by the use of quiet light. The agitation of Perugino's Verrocchiesque training is here suppressed. He models human forms so compactly that he seems to be sealing into each a single intimate, powerful emotion.

ANDREA MANTEGNA. *Judith and Holofernes*

This picture, formerly owned by the Pembroke family, was once in the collection of King Charles I where it was considered to be by Raphael. How it reached the royal collection is unknown, although it has been suggested that this might be the *Judith* attributed to Squarcione in the 1492 Medici inventory made after Lorenzo the Magnificent's death. There is no chronological objection to that hypothesis, for our painting must certainly have been executed by 1492.

The subject was among the artist's favorite themes. The surviving versions include a beautiful drawing dated 1491 in the Uffizi, perhaps a preparatory sketch for an engraving; a pen and charcoal study also in the Uffizi; as well as two monochrome drawings of contested attribution in Montreal and Dublin. There is no doubt that this painting is the most complex and elevated of Mantegna's treatments of the subject. It is incredible that its quality was not appreciated in the 19th century; only in 1918 did Berenson recognize it as autograph, followed subsequently by almost every Mantegna scholar.

The composition is extremely clear and simple. Holofernes' open tent is like a curtain about to descend upon the epilogue of the tragic story. Judith's solemn composure, as she calmly turns her head aside while dropping Holofernes' bloody head into the sack held by a terrified serving woman, speaks of a chasteness and emotional restraint that is truly classic in its poetry.

Although Mantegna's fascination for the antique sometimes approached the dry passion of the archeologist, here he strikes a happy medium. He turned to the classical world not to learn naturalism, but to discover the vocabulary of dignity and gravity. In his great fresco cycles the emotions and intellectual allusions are inspired by more wide ranging interests than mere pedantic interest in the antique.

The small dimensions of this picture favored the delicate, almost miniaturist

ANDREA MANTEGNA
Isola di Carturo 1431 — Mantua 1506
Judith and Holofernes (circa 1490)
Panel; 11 7/8″ × 7 1/8″.
Widener Collection, 1942
(acquired from the Pembroke Collection,
Wilton House, England).

execution of the drapery in Judith's dress, the blue mantle thrown about her, her exotic sandals and the servant's turban. The spirit and subtlety of color accords well with the grace and refinement of what we know concerning Mantegna's lost Vatican frescoes executed between 1488 and 1490 and described by Traja in 1750. They correspond also to the almost calligraphic refinement of the figures in the *Triumphs of Caesar* at Hampton Court, executed between 1484 and 1492 for the court of Mantua. The poor condition of the latter makes it difficult to compare their color with the *Judith,* which is audacious and at the same time restrained, a typical Mantegnesque contrast of yellow and red, accented by the dark background of the tent and of the night sky.

ANTONELLO DA MESSINA. *Madonna and Child*

This is a basic work in the complex evolution of Antonello's style, which was the matured fruit of multiple grafts, rigorously selected and assimilated by his genius and raised to an extremely high stylistic unity.

Comparison with securely attributed works would suggest a date for this masterpiece shortly after 1470. The tight composition of the *Virgin and Child* is pyramidal. The three-quarter pose gives architectonic grandeur to the masses in a luminous space enclosed by the balustrade. The faces and hands have an extraordinary limpid, crystalline clarity. The tender gesture of the smiling child reveals the artist's humanity. The miraculous synthesis of form and light is not far from the *Ecce Homo* of 1470 in New York. In a way, the painting cannot be explained without Antonello's having been acquainted with Piero della Francesca's works in Naples and also perhaps with that elusive French luminist, Enguerrand Quarton, who was active in Provence. The clean structure of the Virgin's forehead and the arch of her eyebrows may also reflect the influence on Antonello of the sculptor Francesco Laurana, active in Sicily in the 1470s.

Later experiments, particularly in color, were to change Antonello's style after 1475, that is, during his Venetian period, when he was influenced by the poetic light of Giovanni Bellini.

GIOVANNI BELLINI. *The Feast of the Gods*   p. 36

Although this beautiful picture is signed and dated 1514, it nonetheless has presented many problems. It is known that it was painted for one of the alabaster rooms in the Castello at Ferrara and that the payments for the picture ended in 1514. But its style leads one to think that it must have been conceived much earlier and that it might be identified with a 1509 project for Isabella d'Este. The left-hand part of the landscape background is Titian's work; he altered the composition about 1530 (R. Pallucchini) to bring the picture into harmony with his own *Bacchanals* which were meant to decorate the same rooms. X-rays reveal that Bellini originally conceived the landscape as a file of trees similar to the *Death of St. Peter Martyr* in London and to other late works, but that it remained incomplete.

This confirms Vasari's statement that the painting was finished by Titian because Bellini was too old and tired. X-rays also reveal Titian's intervention in certain passages of the nymphs' drapery, which were apparently too modest for the tastes of the Ferrarese court. What is extraordinary is

34

ANTONELLO DA MESSINA
Messina 1430 — Messina 1479
Madonna and Child
(datable shortly after 1470)
Panel; 23 1/4″ × 17 1/4″.
Andrew Mellon Collection, 1937.

that Bellini's rich color and complex narrative survived the ardor of Titian's own tumultous landscape style.

The scene depicted is taken from Ovid. A group of gods accompanied by satyrs and nymphs is about to sacrifice an ass. Priapus is attempting to lift the skirts of the sleeping nymph Lotis on the right, but the braying of the ass frustrates his intentions, much to the amusement of the assembled company. The episode is the kind of elegant jest that one would expect of a Humanistic admirer of Lucian.

GIOVANNI BELLINI
Venice circa 1430 — Venice 1516
The Feast of the Gods (1514)
Oil on canvas; 67" × 74". Signed and dated.
Painted for Alfonso I, Duke of Este.
Widener Collection, 1942.

36

Although we lack direct evidence about the formation of Bellini's Humanist style, we can nonetheless reconstruct the intellectual atmosphere in which he lived in his late maturity, the first decade of the 15th century, a glorious moment in Venetian culture. He would have been aware of the writings of such leading figures as Bembo and Manuzio, and of the recovery of the antique literary tradition that had come about through the publications of the Accademia Aldina. This conjunction of influences explains Bellini's turning to Humanist themes, as against his earlier work which was almost exclusively religious.

His spiritual evolution coincides also with the influences Dürer brought to Venice. One sees here echoes of Dürer's *Feast of the Rosary* executed for the church of St. Bartholomew in 1506. Bellini was obviously aware as well of the new vigor Giorgione gave to his own already elaborate colorism and to the younger master's ideas about the mysterious relationships between man and nature.

GIOVANNI BELLINI. *Portrait of a Young Man in Red* p. 37

Except for the almost Botticelli-like lyricism of the Birmingham portrait of a youth, which in any case was executed before 1474, Giovanni Bellini's portraiture after 1475 faithfully follows Antonello da Messina's conception of figures posed three-quarter length and gazing more inwardly upon themselves than out to the spectator. This portrait of a young man is among Bellini's most forceful and personal works.

Bellini expresses his admiration for Antonello's rigorous volumetric composition in the structure of this bust, in the regularity of the drapery and in the parallel edges of the headdress that falls over the sitter's shoulders. The artist has placed nothing between the spectator and the young man who is immersed in an airy atmosphere and set against a luminous sky with puffy clouds. The red of his jacket is like a trumpet blast, as is the splendid self-assurance emanating from his face.

VITTORE CARPACCIO. *The Virgin Reading*

Next to a marble balustrade a young woman in a white turban and a sumptuous pink and orange dress sits reading intently despite the distractions an ample landscape might offer her eye. The halo suggests she is a saint, perhaps St. Catherine of Alexandria. The leg of the Christ Child once visible on the cushion at the left indicates that this is a fragment of a larger composition and makes one think that the figure might be the Virgin reading while the Child played, perhaps with a bird, a flower, a butterfly or a Cross.

Although we may have lost one of Carpaccio's amiable narrative fables, the surviving fragment is enjoyable if only for its rigorous stylistic coherence. The same composition of a woman seated in the right foreground is found in the *Nativity* in the Scuola degli Albanesi series, one of which is dated 1504. It is very probable that the Scuola composition found its prototype in the painting reproduced here, where the Vivarini-like volumes, the stylization of the folds in the sleeve and the sharp division between light and shade on the balustrade suggest a somewhat harder and therefore earlier style. However formally the work is perhaps closer in its simplified composition and clear, hard luminosity to the *Calling of Matthew* in the S. Giorgio degli Schiavoni series, which is datable 1502.

The immobility of the figure is in keeping with the serenity of the landscape. The topography must certainly evoke the white farmlands between mountain and sea on the Dalmatian coast which Carpaccio must have known so well.

VITTORE CARPACCIO
Venice circa 1455 — Venice 1523(?)
The Virgin Reading (circa 1500)
Panel; 30 3/4" × 20".
Formerly in the Benson Collection, London.
Samuel H. Kress Collection, 1939.

LEONARDO DA VINCI. *Ginevra de' Benci*

The young lady is generally identified as the Ginevra de' Benci portrayed by Leonardo, according to old sources, before he left Florence for Milan. However, some scholars attribute the painting to Verrocchio or Lorenzo di Credi. The calm of the sitter does have affinities with the style of these artists, but the elevated poetry of the characterization and the melting of forms into the atmosphere can only be Leonardo's work, contemporary to his *Adoration of the Magi.*

Although the paint surface is well preserved, the painting has lost several inches at the bottom, as the incomplete wreath on the rear of the panel indicates. A drawing in Windsor of a woman's hands is thought to be a preliminary study for the lost part of the picture.

The disposition in space of the three-quarter length figure is masterful. The head is turned slightly towards us, but not full face, so that we can appreciate how the luminous ringlets of hair curl tightly around the head and soften the face. The subtly modeled face is set against a dark clump of juniper trees (a pun on Ginevra's name) which allows a soft light to filter in on the left and affords, on the right, a view of a landscape not as heroic as that in the *Virgin of the Rocks,* but already suffused with a rare poetry. The mask-like face of the young woman, while lacking the fascinating ambiguity of the *Mona Lisa,* breathes equivocation and mystery.

The painting until recently had belonged for several centuries to the Princes of Liechtenstein. It was in their Viennese palace that Waagen saw the picture in 1866 and first pronounced it to be a Leonardo. For half a century following, experts argued the case until Adolfo Venturi and Berenson polarized opinion in the proper direction. The recent clamor when the painting passed to America at least found critics agreed on the attribution of this precious portrait to Leonardo.

RAPHAEL. *St. George and the Dragon*   *p. 42*

This is Raphael's second and more mature treatment of the theme, the first being the slightly earlier and better known Louvre picture which critics generally think was executed in 1505 at the latest. This painting was done about 1506 during a visit to his native Urbino and was commissioned by Duke Guidobaldo da Montefeltro. Along with the *St. Michael* and *St. George* in the Louvre plus the Chantilly *Three Graces,* it is one of Raphael's youthful *"poesie."*

One can see in the landcape the artist's renewed contacts with the Umbrian countryside. Nonetheless, the composition is much more arranged than in

LEONARDO DA VINCI
Vinci 1452 — Amboise 1519
Ginevra de' Benci (circa 1481)
Panel; 15 1/8″ × 14 1/2″.
National Gallery of Art purchase, 1967.

the Louvre *St. George,* in the definition of planes, for instance, in the distribution of masses and voids, in the play of diagonals which resolve into an X. While one can speak of arrangement and planning, it was actually Raphael's instinctive preference for harmonious composition that led his hand to structure the picture in this way.

Raphael's personality is also evident in the way the joyous, victorious elements of the narrative predominate over the grotesque and monstrous. In a clear morning light our attention is centered on the snowy white horse whose plasticity may reflect the influence of Leonardo, but whose almost human glance back towards the spectator is reminiscent of ancient Homeric or medieval legends.

42

RAPHAEL
Urbino 1483 — Rome 1520
St. George and the Dragon (1505–1506)
Panel; 11 1/8″ × 8 3/8″. Signed.
Commissioned by Guidobaldo da
Montefeltro, Duke of Urbino,
for Henry VII of England.
Andrew Mellon Collection, 1937.

RAPHAEL.   *The Alba Madonna*

The painting is considered among Raphael's most exalted, echoing the elevated spiritualism of the Vatican Stanza della Segnatura, which was completed in 1512. The similarities between the Virgin here and Michelangelo's 1508–1509 *Sibyls* in the Sistine ceiling document Raphael's fascination with Michelangelo's work.

The tender passivity of the *Virgin with the Goldfinch* and the *Belle Jardinière* has been superseded here by a psychological tension hinting at fore-

bodings and defensiveness. The pyramidal composition that served in earlier pictures to insert the group securely in space recurs, but now suggests instability and motion. However Raphael's preference for solid forms prevails. A particularly Michelangelesque motif is the Child with his limbs thrown out and firmly clutching the Cross.

The amber flesh tones harmonize with the delicate blues of the Virgin's draperies. The prevailing blues link the foreground with the far distance, and the over-all silvery tone creates a limpid atmosphere that enshrouds objects and people.

RAPHAEL. *Bindo Altoviti*

A review of Raphael's portraiture, from his now ruined Uffizi *Self-Portrait* to the Pitti triple portrait of Leo X, would be enough to illustrate the evolution of the artist's personality and style. He was a masterful interpreter of human nature, capable of synthesizing in a portrait both the physical and spiritual character of a sitter, nuances of expression, rank and cultivation. While in his youth he may have assimilated elements of Leonardo's style and been influenced by Northern conventions, later he created his own individual portrait technique.

The portrait of Bindo Altoviti is a fine example from his late maturity, of the time of the Farnesina *Galatea* and the Vatican *Fire in the Borgo*. The sitter is generally identified as the Florentine banker who commissioned Raphael's *Madonna of the Veil*. In the portrait we are struck not only by the beauty of the sitter but also by his vitality. Nothing distracts attention from the figure who seems to turn towards us while walking. He is set against a chill green background, like those found in paintings by the young Lotto or in Northern portraits.

Leonardesque shadows intensify the expression of the firmly drawn face. The Venetian colorism, learned from Sebastiano del Piombo, is confined to the rich drapery. The light aids in modeling the sensual face and hair and lightly touches the hand. But the most important art-historical quality of the portrait, in terms of the development of Mannerism, is the suggestion of a fascinating and transient apparition.

GIORGIONE. *The Adoration of the Shepherds*   *pp. 46–47*

Before the mouth of a cave in which animals are barely discerned, the kneeling Madonna has, as in analogous German and Flemish scenes, improvised a cushion for the Child from a portion of her mantle. Two poor shepherds, answering the mysterious summons, have come to contemplate the Child. In the background, St. Joseph prays. The only indication of the sacredness of the event is the apparition of several cherubs' heads. The cave

RAPHAEL
Bindo Altoviti (circa 1513)
Panel; 23 1/2″ × 17 1/4″.
Commissioned by the banker Bindo Altoviti in whose Florentine palace it remained until the beginning of the 19th century.
Samuel H. Kress Collection, 1943.

of Bethlehem has been transported to the quiet Venetian countryside, certainly not far from Castelfranco where green hills relieve the view and match the blue profile of the distant Alps. As beautiful as the landscape is, it remains only a background to the human narrative.

There is nothing spectacular in the painting. Every element is subordinated to an ideal Christian contemplation and united in a closed, simple composition.

This masterpiece is a recent addition to the list of Giorgione's works. Berenson, dissenting from the attribution to the end of his life, was constrained to create a special master for this work alone, as an attribution to any other known contemporary cannot be sustained. It is very probable that this is the "beautiful and singular scene" that Taddeo Albano, a man in the confidence of Isabella d'Este, described in 1510 as belonging to Vittorio Beccaro. (The Vienna version is perhaps "the not very perfect one" also cited by Albano as belonging to Taddeo Contarini.) The various dates proposed fall in the half decade 1505–1510. Considering its many borrowings from Northern painting, the persistence of a Bellini-like linearism, and finally the refined yet still meticulous and descriptive coloring, it is reasonable to assume that this painting is not a collaborative work and is much closer to the Castelfranco altarpiece than to the *Tempesta,* where Giorgione achieved his revolution in uniting figure and landscape in one mysterious atmosphere.

GIORGIONE
Castelfranco 1477(?) — Venice 1510
The Adoration of the Shepherds (circa 1505)
Panel; 35 3/4" × 43 1/2".
Known as the "Allendale Adoration" after
the London collector who formerly owned it.
Samuel H. Kress Collection, 1939.

TITIAN.   *Venus with a Mirror*   p. 48
Of the numerous versions of the theme, this is the first and the one most likely to be autograph. Its well-established provenance (from Titian's son, Pomponio Vecellio, to the Barbarigo family to Czar Nicholas I) leads one

to suppose that the artist was particularly attached to the painting; at any event he kept it for himself until his death.

It is earlier than the master's late works whose loose and painterly style puzzled Titian's contemporaries but which are much admired today for their spontaneity and drama. The *Venus with a Mirror* falls in the middle of the 1550s; she is a sister to the Prado *Danae* (1554). Venus' sumptuous charm exceeds the classical canon, but is typically 16th century. The juxtaposition of luminous flesh, tawny fur and red velvet with lights like embers creates a sensual mood that is heightened by the almost suffocating atmosphere of marvelous color.

TITIAN. *Doge Andrea Gritti*

It is not certain, but this may be an idealized posthumous portrait of Andrea Gritti executed after his death in 1538 at the age of 83 and meant to commemorate the Doge's indomitable spirit in the difficult times of Venice's battles on land and sea.

The picture may not be the one cited in the collection of King Charles I, and the signature is doubtful. However there is no doubt that it is Titian's

JACOPO TINTORETTO
Venice 1518 — Venice 1594
Christ at the Sea of Galilee (about 1560)
Canvas; 46″ × 66 1/4″.
Samuel H. Kress Collection, 1952.

work, stupendous in its psychological intensity and in the power of the color to underline and reinforce the mood.

The imposing figure is seen with his body turned toward the right while his head is swung proudly to the left, a Mannerist play of torsions that suggests movement. The hand in the foreground energetically grasps the folds of cloth, just as the St. John the Baptist in the Accademia grips his cane and scroll. The figure here is like an inert version of the *Goliath* now in the ceiling of the sacristy of S. Maria della Salute but begun in 1542 for S. Spirito.

The painting reflects the culmination of Titian's Mannerist period in which his genius found new solutions to extend the profundity of his style. The color, akin to the great *Ecce Homo* in Vienna, is one of the most important examples of Titian's colorism, especially considering the perfect condition of the picture which has not even been lined.

JACOPO TINTORETTO. *Christ at the Sea of Galilee*
The painting illustrates an episode in the life of Christ recounted with slight variations by Matthew, Mark and John. While Christ meditated after the miracle of the loaves and fishes, the Apostles embarked at his order for the other bank of the Sea of Galilee. All three Evangelists agree that a violent storm arose on the sea and that Christ appeared to the passengers of the endangered boat. Matthew adds that Peter dared Christ to prove his power by enabling him, too, to walk upon the waters. It is this moment of natural and psychological tension that Tintoretto, an attentive reader in search of new subject matter, chooses to illustrate.

The violent expressionism of the composition has led some students to think the artist was El Greco, Tintoretto's most gifted spiritual heir, but the suggestion is difficult to support. Closest to El Greco's poetry are the white clouds in the dark sky, almost a reproduction in negative of the apocalyptic skies in the *Madonna dell'Orto.*

It is difficult to know where to place the work chronologically in the artist's career, for while it seems a very mature work, there are passages, such as the figures in the boat, that appear closer to Tintoretto's early period. A reasonable dating would place it between the violently drawn and colored *Evangelists* completed in 1557 in S. Maria del Giglio and Tintoretto's articulately linear treatment of figures in the large canvases of the *Madonna dell'Orto.* The elongation of the flying figures at the tops of those canvases, executed about 1560, greatly resembles the figure of Christ here, who calls Peter to prove his faith. The blue-green color used both in sky and sea is also typical of Tintoretto.

PAOLO VERONESE. *The Finding of Moses*

Although there are many versions of this theme in various museums (Madrid, Dresden, Dijon), only this one and the Prado's are recognized as autograph. Iconographically the two versions are practically identical. The composition unwinds, with a wonderful contrapuntal colorism, along a continuous line from the Negro page with the basket and the lady in waiting who hands the infant up to Pharaoh's daughter. On the right, three other figures repeat the theme with a tighter rhythm, the last being a clownish dwarf whose ugliness points up the princess' beauty.

One can guess that the bank falls to the river on the left from the two figures posed on steps. The immediate landscape setting is simply two unidentifiable trees that resemble stage sets, much like those in the Palazzo Ducale *Rape of Europa,* a picture which has the same purely decorative dance-like figures. Beyond the arch of a bridge Veronese has created a fantastic Egyptian city, drawn from his early frescoes. Perhaps this was initially a view of Rome transformed by the fantasy of an Emilian Mannerist.

In comparison with the Madrid version, this painting has a more lively spring in the servant's affectionate haste to cover the foundling and in the princess' beautiful movement towards the child, so like a similar gesture in the *Venus and Mars* in the Metropolitan Museum, New York. It is difficult to decide which is the prototype. In any case, the date of these two works, placed variously by scholars between 1570 and 1580, would seem to be closer to 1580. Such glistening color was something that emerged from the Accademia *Marriage of St. Catherine* of 1575 and the already-mentioned Metropolitan allegory, contemporary to the series painted between 1576 and 1584 for Rudolph II.

The small proportions of the picture afforded Veronese an opportunity to paint an almost postage-stamp size picture in comparison to the scale of his huge decorative cycles and to render once again light and color with a preciousness reminiscent of his Mannerist training.

ALESSANDRO MAGNASCO. *The Baptism of Christ*   p. 54

This and its pendant, *Christ at the Sea of Galilee,* are late works, ca. 1730, certainly from the artist's last period, when he returned to Genoa at almost 70 years of age. The style suggests that date, as well as the use of the theme simply as a pretext for a fantastic landscape. The figures are literally absorbed in nature, if nature is the word one can use to describe this conglomeration of branches, rocks, waves and clouds. Figures are reduced to nervous arabesques that nonetheless reveal a subtle knowledge of anatomy, and objects are rendered with a touch that seems like the lash of a whip. It is just as useless to seek a correspondence here between the Baptism theme and the setting as it is vain to attempt to find a documentary value in Magnasco's hallucinatory scenes of monastic congregations and unrestrained bacchanals.

PAOLO VERONESE
Verona 1528 — Venice 1588
The Finding of Moses (circa 1575–1580)
Canvas; 22 3/4″ × 17 1/2″.
Andrew Mellon Collection, 1937.

Magnasco transforms the theme into a nocturnal, delirious, malignant and obsessive fantasy. But everything is touched with his scintillating technique that extracts the most capricious chromatic juices from the Genoese and Lombard Baroque, a technique that has led him to be mistaken, like Guardi, for a forerunner of Impressionism.

CANALETTO.   *The Portello and the Brenta Canal at Padua*

A thematic change occurred in Canaletto's work about 1740. The output of Venetian views decreased and the number of mainland scenes increased, particularly views of the famous Brenta Canal that reaches Padua near the Portello. Several influences brought this about. First, the war of the

54

ALESSANDRO MAGNASCO
Genoa 1667 — Genoa 1749
The Baptism of Christ (circa 1730)
Canvas; 46 1/4″ × 57 3/4″.
Samuel H. Kress Collection, 1943.

Austrian Succession broke out in 1741 and must certainly have reduced the number of those visitors to Venice who bought Canaletto's pictures as souvenirs. Also Canaletto apparently went to Rome a second time in 1742, for the Roman views dated 1742 and 1743 have a pictorial sense and tonality that would have been impossible for the artist to recreate entirely from memories of his first trip in 1719. Finally, the marvelous engravings, first produced out of economic necessity, became a vehicle for the contemplative melancholy that so enriched Canaletto's vocabulary.

It was at this moment in his poetic development that this great view reproduced here was created. There are two preparatory studies for the picture: one in Windsor Castle, much reduced and with a different viewpoint; the other in the Albertina, closer to the finished composition, but with the view slightly less extended at the sides. The scene is bathed in the same warm light of the Roman views already cited. The space given over to blue sky delicately touched with lilac-grey clouds is slightly larger than the area occupied by the ruined quays of hot brick between which projects the white stone of the Portello gate. The boats, the women with children and the cavaliers on the bridge fail to animate the scene, which, despite its serene light, is vaguely melancholy.

CANALETTO
Venice 1679 — Venice 1768
The Portello and the Brenta Canal at Padua
(1735–1740?)
Canvas; 24 5/8″ × 43″.
Samuel H. Kress Collection, 1961.

PIETRO LONGHI. *Blindman's Buff* p. 56

The simple, almost timid composition and the coloristic refinement of every detail, as festive as a painting by Liotard, make one think that this delightful scene belongs to the beginning of Longhi's middle period. With exquisite sensibility, both as narrator and painter, Longhi describes the innocent amusements and little intrigues that take place during a visit to a middle-class home. There is no sense of his judging and much less of his commenting ironically on the society he describes.

While the seated man is amused at the boy's attempt to break the pot, impeded as he is by a blindfold and a multicolored apron, a bored and distracted young lady seems impatiently to wait a word from the elegant cavalier at her side.

The dark green wall covering creates an intimate atmosphere. On the table, covered by a pink cloth, are seen goblets, bottles and pastries.

FRANCESCO GUARDI. *Campo San Zanipolo*

The festive Rococo staircase seen in front of the arcaded Renaissance façade of the Scuola di S. Marco was a temporary structure raised during the visit of Pope Pius VI to Venice. From the top of these stairs the Pope

FRANCESCO GUARDI
Venice 1712 — Venice 1793
Campo San Zanipolo (1782)
Detail.
Canvas; 14 3/4″ × 12 3/8″.
One of a series commissioned by Pietro Edwards of the ceremonies in honor of Pope Pius VI.
Samuel H. Kress Collection, 1939.

PIETRO LONGHI
Venice 1702 — Venice 1785
Blindman's Buff (about 1745)
Canvas; 19 1/4″ × 24″.
Formerly in the
Giovannelli collection, Venice.
Samuel H. Kress Collection, 1939.

blessed the crowd assembled in the square. The pontiff's visit was commemorated in a series of documentary paintings commissioned from Guardi by the city government through the Inspector of Arts, Pietro Edwards. This picture repeats, in a simplified manner, the central motif of one of those pictures, now in the Bearsted Collection, Upton House.

The eye-level is fixed at the door of the church of S. Zanipolo; the picturesque square lies behind the viewer's shoulder. A few of the crowd have lingered after the ceremony. The extraordinary mobility of light and shadow,

GIOVANNI BATTISTA TIEPOLO
Venice 1696 — Venice 1770
Apollo Pursuing Daphne (1765–1766?)
Canvas; 27″ × 34 1/4″.
Samuel H. Kress Collection, 1952.

58

the scintillating decorative details glittering on the Renaissance façade seem still to reverberate noise and bustle.

Francesco Guardi's documentary paintings, enlivening history as they do with such lyric effusion, were always considered something curious. The late appreciation of their quality is owing to the series of views engraved by Brustolon. It is particularly in these paintings that Guardi's full genius is to be seen because such documentary views became exercises for his fervid evocative fantasy. What they actually record is the inventive qualities of this topological poet.

GIOVANNI BATTISTA TIEPOLO.   *Apollo Pursuing Daphne*
The painting is a pendant to *Venus and Vulcan* in the Johnson Collection, Philadelphia; until 1873 both were in the Gsell Collection, Vienna, where they were considered overdoor decorations. There is a precise compositional relationship between the two; each has an oblique but inverse diagonal symmetry separating the elements of the composition. Here the axis begins in the dark pines on the left, descends along the rosy nude and continues into an illuminated zone that contrasts with the woody mass. All this forms a closed group with Daphne backed towards the river god, her father, who has arrived only just in time to save his daughter. Behind them cowers Cupid, who was responsible for the whole story.

There is a painting of the same theme in the Louvre, more satisfying only in the treatment of the figure of Apollo; the years separating the two versions brought a greater refinement, especially of color, to Tiepolo's style. His capacity to imprison light in color flowers particularly at this moment of his career, after the superb Würzburg cycle (1752). The stepped composition is also typical of this later period. The simple structure, the airy unfolding of forms in space, the taste for clear color saturated with light can be compared with his frescoes in Villa Valmarana, Vicenza (1757): *Venus Abandoning Aeneas, Apollo and Diana* and others.

Using what was for him a relatively small canvas and liberated here from the technical limitations of frescoing by the use of oil paint, Tiepolo was able to cast his Daphne as a splendid nude, full of light, in a hot afternoon atmosphere. Only Fragonard at this time could have painted a female nude with as much fragrance. But in contrast to Fragonard's upholstered alcoves, this nymph is framed in a paradisical landscape perfectly appropriate to the solar myth.

AMEDEO MODIGLIANI.   *Gypsy Woman with Baby*   *p. 60*
A young woman with a shuttered expression and melancholy eyes sits with her baby bundled in a dark wrap in her arms. Only a pink cheek of the

child can be seen beneath his droll cap. Perhaps a social protest lies at the root of this picture, but if so, it is mellowed by the lyricism of the eternal mother and child theme. This is a late work in the burning parabola of Modigliani's stylistic development, and the language is one of simplified forms, color and line.

60

AMEDEO MODIGLIANI
Livorno 1884 — Paris 1920
Gypsy Woman with Baby (1918)
Canvas; 25 3/4" × 39 3/4".
Chester Dale Collection, 1962.

FRANCE

FRANÇOIS CLOUET. *Diane de Poitiers*

The painting, signed on the edge of the tub, beneath the beringed hand of the beauty, probably dates from about 1571, the period of the Louvre portrait of Elizabeth of Austria, for which there is a dated drawing, and which has a rather similar hair style. The sitter in our portrait has been identified as Diane de Poitiers (1499–1566), mistress of Henry II and of whom there are various other likenesses. It is noteworthy that there is only one other signed Clouet portrait, that of his friend the pharmacist, P. Quthe.

The portrait is typical of the Fontainebleau School which followed the custom of representing women in their baths, an obvious allusion to an antique Venus theme. In this instance there are probably other hidden literary references. On one level the picture seems to be almost an allegory of fertility; on another, the artist certainly must have wished to juxtapose the rustic warmth and solidity of the nurse with the Junoesque sophistication and marble-like coldness of the self-possessed lady who is animated by only a shiver of pride. She is detached from the spectator, while the serving maid, by contrast, winks at you.

The rest of the scene follows a convention; the background is a corner of a chamber with a lighted fire. There is a glimpse of a piece of tapestried furniture decorated with a unicorn, the courtly symbol of chastity.

This portrait type, which became the fashion in artistocratic circles, is pleasing for its intimate view into the daily life of the sitters. Antoine Caron and François Quesnel painted such pictures, as well as a number of anonymous artists.

The painting shows the meeting of two traditions. It has a Flemish taste for genre detail and overtones of Italian Mannerism in the conception of the main figure, with its evocation of Bronzino's and Giovanni da Bologna's sophistication.

FRANÇOIS CLOUET
Tours circa 1510 — Paris 1572
Diane de Poitiers (circa 1571)
Panel; 36 1/4" × 32".
Samuel H. Kress Collection, 1961
Inscribed: "FR. IANETII OPVS"

LOUIS LE NAIN. *Landscape with Peasants*

The scene depicts the artist's native Picardy, even to the silvery color of the atmosphere.

In the shade of a high wall, like a stage set, an old woman sits on the left watching several children, perhaps her grandchildren, standing in the foreground on the threshold of the picture, as if posing for a group photograph — a typical Le Nain arrangement. Behind this domestic scene, a kind of peasant elegy that is a precursor of 19th-century Naturalism, particularly Corot's, opens an immense landscape where sky and earth meet in the far distance, banded by the long shadows that precede sunset.

The brothers Antoine, Louis, and Mathieu Le Nain, from Laon, lived and worked together in Paris from 1630 onwards. It is difficult to distinguish their separate hands in the paintings that issued from their workshop. Mathieu was a portraitist influenced by Caravaggio. Antoine was more old-fashioned and liked brilliant colors. It was Louis who created these rural elegies where the characters, without betraying anything of their peasant origins, seem to approach the spectator with the calm curiosity of country folk watching a stranger pass.

Louis Le Nain's work is the antithesis of the Classical trend in French painting represented by Poussin, Bourdon and La Hyre. That classical style was the art of the court and in the second half of the 17th century inspired Lebrun's academic Baroque, the official style of the reign of Louis XIV. Though Le Nain's dignified realism affected French 18th-century painting, specifically Chardin, it remained a kind of oasis in the official culture of the time and had close affinities not with French but with Dutch painting. In fact, the present landscape is worthy of van Goyen, but in Louis Le Nain's hands is endowed with a sweet and intense humanity. The theme of his work is the rapport between man and nature as seen in the lives of simple folk. It is probably the most serious product of the 17th-century genre tradition.

LOUIS LE NAIN
Laon circa 1593 — Paris 1648
Landscape with Peasants (circa 1640)
Oil on canvas; 18 3/8" × 22 1/2".
Samuel H. Kress Collection, 1946.

NICOLAS POUSSIN. *The Assumption of the Virgin*

Two darkly fluted columns rise against the sky on the left and right. Beneath is the simple form of a sarcophagus from which is tumbled a white shroud. This is the static frame that gives impulse to the Virgin's ascent. The composition is not unlike the Louvre's *Delivery of St. Peter,* also by Poussin.

Its affinities with Guercino places the work, of which there are several recorded versions, in the master's Venetian phase, that is, in the 1620s when the artist first came to Italy and settled in Rome.

The miracle is treated in the dramatic vocabulary of the Baroque, yet the architectural setting is severely restrained. It is no mere theatrical backdrop, as in most 17th-century painting, but an expressive module that evokes with unusual rigor the severity of the antique.

NICOLAS POUSSIN
Les Andelys 1594 — Rome 1665
The Assumption of the Virgin
(circa 1626)
Oil on canvas; 52 7/8″ × 38 5/8″.
Ailsa Mellon Bruce Fund, 1963.

CLAUDE LORRAIN
(CLAUDE GELLÉE)
Chamagne 1600 — Rome 1682
The Herdsman (circa 1635)
Oil on canvas; 47 3/4″ × 63 1/8″.
Samuel H. Kress Collection, 1946.

CLAUDE LORRAIN. *The Herdsman*

Executed between 1655 and 1660, the painting is as rich and subtle as a symphony. The *corpus* of Claude's work reveals an intense, coherent interior vision of an ideal landscape. It is the countryside around Rome, ennobled and treated as a charming idyll. Claude expanded the earlier Classicizing landscape tradition of Annibale Carracci into a sublime image of nature, his art reaching a peak in the 1650s when it approached the synthesis of his countryman and friend, Nicolas Poussin.

The moment is mid-afternoon; the sun floods everything in a golden haze. A river winds into the distance. On the left, a shepherd takes refuge beneath the trees while his flock grazes in the dazzling light.

67

ANTOINE WATTEAU. *Italian Comedians*

Watteau was the first and perhaps the most remarkable of Rococo painters. During his life, the importance of Versailles as the center of official French art during the reign of Louis XIV declined and the sophisticated salons of Paris became the focus of the art world. Watteau's painting embodies the quintessence of the Rococo. It is no accident that the artist began as a collaborator of Claude Audran, executing those delicious grotesques, halfway between late Mannerism and Chinoiserie, destined to decorate the intimate cabinets of Parisian houses.

The singular combination of stylistic elements in Watteau's art make him an important protagonist of French art in the first 20 years of the 18th century. Besides his training in a decorator's studio, where the Rococo was born and later adapted to the so-called fine arts, his roots lay also in the North; in fact he came from the Hainault region which was part of the Low Countries until 1678. In Watteau's hands the Northern genre tradition, popularized by such painters as van Ostade and Teniers, was given a sentimental brio when it came into contact with the worldliness of Europe's first city.

A handful of Watteau's works depict theatrical subjects, reflecting the artist's literary interests as well as his collaboration between 1703 and 1708 with the stage-set painter for the company of Italian actors in Paris, Claude Gillot (1663–1721). Here Watteau came by his repertory of debonaire themes, then so popular, and especially of Commedia dell'Arte characters.

Besides our painting, Watteau's most famous pictures of actors are the *Harlequin, Pierrot and Scapin* at Althorp, *Love at the French Theater* and *Love at the Italian Theater,* both in Berlin, *The French Comedians* in New York and the Louvre's *Gilles.* In addition to this series there is another one of allegorical representations of contemporary figures in actors' costumes. Though they have the same gallant air, they, like this work, are difficult to interpret.

It has been suggested that this picture was done for Watteau's personal physician, Richard Mead, in 1720, shortly before the artist's death; and indeed the painting is full of melancholy.

The troupe of Italian actors was disbanded in 1697 following the closing of their theater on the orders of the puritanical Mme. de Maintenon, last favorite of Louis XIV. However, it was reconstituted in 1716 through the intervention of that gay regent, the Duke d'Orléans.

ANTOINE WATTEAU
Valenciennes 1684 — Valenciennes 1721
Italian Comedians (probably 1720)
Oil on canvas; 25 1/8″ × 30″.
Samuel H. Kress Collection, 1946.

ANTOINE WATTEAU
Sylvia (circa 1720)
Oil on canvas; 27 1/4″ × 23 1/8″.
Samuel H. Kress Collection, 1946.

ANTOINE WATTEAU. *Sylvia*

A draftsman even in his youth, when he was particularly impressed by the acrobats he saw at country fairs, Watteau later copied paintings for art dealers and collaborated in executing theater sets with Gillot and Chinoiserie decorations with Audran. But he found his own mature style only after his exposure to the Rubens series in Marie de' Medici's Luxembourg palace, of which Audran was in charge.

This stupendous portrait shows such a fusion of styles that Delacroix called it "a synthesis of Venice and Flanders."

JEAN–BAPTISTE–SIMÉON CHARDIN. *The House of Cards*

There are various treatments of this theme, other than this autograph picture of about 1735, in which a youth builds imaginary castles of folded cards upon a green topped table. With such realistic subjects from everyday life Chardin could at once satisfy the Rococo taste for the graceful, and also follow those moralizing tendencies in which he had Diderot's support. Such paintings as this are a link between the Le Nain brothers and Corot. They avoid the gallant and frivolous arcadian conceits of his contemporaries Watteau and Boucher. For all its upper-class connotation and grace, such a picture is the beginning of an art of social commitment.

70

JEAN–BAPTISTE–SIMÉON CHARDIN
Paris 1699 — Paris 1779
The House of Cards (circa 1735)
Oil on canvas; 32 3/8″ × 26″. Signed.
Andrew Mellon Collection, 1937.

FRANÇOIS BOUCHER
Paris 1703 — Paris 1770
Allegory of Music (1764)
Oil on canvas; 40 3/4" × 51 1/8".
Signed and dated.
Samuel H. Kress Collection, 1946.

FRANÇOIS BOUCHER. *Allegory of Music*

Boucher was educated first as a decorator (his father executed designs for embroideries) and then was influenced by Lemoyne, La Fosse and Coypel, which explains the exquisite lightness and decorative quality that flowered in such works as this one. He traveled to Rome with Charles van Loo and on returning had a great success in court circles. The 1737 Salon marked the apogee of his career and the beginning of his mature style. Patronized by Mme. de Pompadour, Boucher found his niche as the director of the Gobelins tapestry works. It was he who carried on the tradition of the court painter begun by Charles Lebrun under Louis XIV.

The *Allegory of Music* and its pendant, *Allegory of Painting,* are examples of the manner that made Boucher the successor to Watteau as the painter of gallant themes. The wide range of light colors, pale reflections of Rubens' opulent palette, are characteristic. His repertory of subjects was vast, but he was most at home in mythologies and allegories. His protagonist is always a young, elegant and sensually abandoned woman. Through Boucher's painting, such a smiling beauty became the symbol of the reign of Louis XV.

JEAN–MARC NATTIER
Paris 1685 — Paris 1766
Mme. de Caumartin as Hebe (1753)
Oil on canvas; 40 3/8" × 32".
Samuel H. Kress Collection, 1946.
Signed and dated: "Nattier pinxit. / 1753."

JEAN–HONORÉ FRAGONARD
Grasse 1732 — Paris 1806
A Young Girl Reading (circa 1776)
Oil on canvas; 32" × 25 1/2".
Gift of Mrs. Mellon Bruce
in memory of her
father Andrew Mellon, 1961.

JEAN–MARC NATTIER. *Mme. de Caumartin as Hebe*

Nattier began his career as an official portraitist in 1742 by depicting a daughter of Louis XV, Mme. Henriette, as Flora — a nymph wearing a crown of flowers. Thus he introduced, along with Falconet in sculpture, a type of allegorical portrait, such as this one, in which the sitter is presented in semi-mythological costume as the wine-bearer to the gods. The finesse of such a flattering notion enjoyed a great vogue in the 18th century.

JEAN–HONORÉ FRAGONARD. *A Young Girl Reading*

This painting of about 1776 is justly famous both for the intimate and penetrating treatment of the theme as well as for the freshness and vivacity of execution. The brushwork has a freedom and virtuosity that is redolent of the Rococo. A few colors have been brilliantly worked to achieve a rich and luminous effect. The pose is simple and the painting is unencumbered with ornament. Here Fragonard combines the qualities of Boucher and Chardin in a way that seems to be a distant precursor of the Impressionists. Nonetheless, Fragonard's fame in the 18th century rested on his decorative and gallant works and not on this profound aspect of his art.

73

JEAN–AUGUSTE–DOMINIQUE INGRES. *Mme. Moitessier*

"An artist's pencil was never entrusted the task of reproducing features more beautiful, more splendid, more superb, more Junoesque." So the poet Théophile Gautier wrote of Mme. Moitessier. Ingres agreed to portray her in 1844, after much perplexity and indecision, presaging the long agony the project would give the artist because of his dissatisfaction and scruples. He worked on the portrait seven years, finishing it only in 1851, but even then he seemed dissatisfied, for he immediately began a second version, now in the National Gallery, London, which was completed only in 1856. As was his habit, Ingres made many preparatory studies for the over-all composition and for details, documenting the long process of his search for perfection.

The second, London portrait is even more sumptuous than this version. There the figure is seated and the entire lower part of the picture is given over to a dress that is a froth of flowers. A mirror in the background reflects the sitter's profile and soft, fleshy shoulders.

The Washington portrait is more restrained, but does not lack that opulence characteristic of the bourgeoisie in the Second Empire. The standing figure in dark velvet dominates a space into which only a few objects of decor intrude. Her jewels, flowers, lace and slightly roseate flesh shimmer against the dark dress and background. One notices certain daring deformations that the purity and elevation of the style absorb and completely justify, for instance the "impossible" anatomical relationship between the left arm and shoulder. The delicately articulated right hand lightly holding the pearl necklace is like an Ingres hallmark, expressing his love for the ideal that permeates the almost architectural composure of the face gazing out at us with enigmatic fixity.

JEAN–BAPTISTE–CAMILLE COROT. *Agostina*   p. 76

When Corot died in 1875, aged 79, the huge crowd following his funeral was an expression of how well the artist was known and loved. However his contemporaries' limited knowledge of his art is revealed by the fact that many paintings, especially his figure pieces that were in no way inferior to the famous, large landscapes, remained unknown until 30 years later when they were exhibited at the Salon d'Automne in 1909. *Agostina,* ca. 1866, is one such masterpiece, painted at a time when Corot frequently did figure paintings such as the stylistically analogous *Interrupted Letter* in Chicago or the Kröller-Müller *Young Woman at the Well.* The figure almost obscures the landscape, but the passage is none the less essential to the picture's serene harmony which is based on a fine balance of elements.

JEAN–AUGUSTE-DOMINIQUE INGRES
Montauban 1780 — Paris 1867
Mme. Moitessier (1851)
Oil on canvas; 57 3/4" × 39 1/2".
Inscribed at upper right:
"M͏ᴱ INNES MOITESSIER / NÉE DE FOUCAULD."
At middle left:
"I.A.D. INGRES PˣIT ANᴼ 1851."
Samuel H. Kress Collection, 1946.

It was Corot's method, a self-discipline that became almost a fixation, to take into careful consideration the proportion and preponderance of the elements of his composition and their sometimes seemingly insignificant relationships to each other. The picture thus became a kind of organism much richer than the simple and easily comprehended views they may at first glance seem to be. The small formats he generally favored permitted the artist to extract a maximum value from each brush stroke, particularly how lights and shadows should be placed to create the most sensitive contrasts. However his vision in small canvases did not change in such large-scale pieces as this picture, so ignored by critics.

Corot's neatness, freshness and the meticulous appropriateness of each stroke, his delicate passages of impasto describing polished flesh tones, are well seen in *Agostina*. But amid all this, the sense of the figure's movement is never submerged; she is beautifully balanced before a landscape that records Corot's love of serenity and of the Italian vision.

JEAN–BAPTISTE–CAMILLE COROT
Paris 1796 — Paris 1875
Agostina (circa 1866)
Oil on canvas; 52 1/8″ × 38 3/8″.
Signed at lower left.
Chester Dale Collection, 1962.

JEAN–BAPTISTE–CAMILLE COROT
Forest of Fontainebleau (circa 1830)
Oil on canvas; 69 1/8″ × 95 1/2″.
Signed at lower left.
Chester Dale Collection, 1962.

JEAN–BAPTISTE–CAMILLE COROT.   *Forest of Fontainebleau*

One of the first critics to recognize Corot's pre-eminence as a landscape painter was Baudelaire who in 1845 said that the artist would be the master of an entire younger generation. Baudelaire's opinion and indeed Corot's great success was based on pictures such as this one. Only after his death did the public learn of those figure paintings the artist kept hidden in his studio, believing that they would not be well received. If we nowadays tend to esteem these "secret" pictures as his masterpieces, we should not overlook the genius in Corot's "public" paintings. This sumptuous landscape is the heir of a long European tradition and not unmarked by the conventions of contemporaneous Romanticism. Still, certain transparent passages, subtle harmonies and areas of light bespeak Corot's new way of seeing and prophetic modernity.

77

GUSTAVE COURBET. *The Grotto of the Loue*

"The most elemental and fertile forms and appearances of the world, its simple and immense primordial forces were selected and absorbed by Courbet," writes Ragghianti, ". . . he achieved an extraordinary change, even in his creative technique, reaching a power and force that is unclassifiable in terms of any other earlier painting." It is a good description for the solemn dark of this grotto that loses itself in black obscurity after the last notes of light fade on the water. Here, as in many other Courbet paintings, there is a "magical and bottomless" peace that no explanation or literary interpretation is capable of disturbing. Every allusion and memory is canceled out in the human fullness that is Courbet's art. It is an art full of vital juices, sustained by its own ample substance, rich in contrast and light, shorn of distracting elements.

GUSTAVE COURBET
Ornans 1819 — Vevey 1877
The Grotto of the Loue (circa 1865)
Oil on canvas; 38 3/4" × 51 3/8".
Signed at lower left.
Gift of Charles L. Lindemann, 1957.

HONORÉ DAUMIER
Marseilles 1808 — Valmondois 1879
Advice to a Young Artist (1855–1860)
Oil on canvas; 16 1/8″ × 12 7/8″:
Signed at lower left.
Gift of Duncan Phillips, 1941.

HONORÉ DAUMIER.   *Advice to a Young Artist*

Like other print-makers in times past and present, it has been Daumier's lot that his painted works have been submerged beneath the enormous volume of his graphic art. It has been estimated that he produced something like 5,000 lithographs in contrast to the approximately 300 paintings and 150 water colors now known. This relatively modest *corpus* is all that remains after the laborious pruning of the numerous spurious attributions that sprouted up as the prices his works commanded rose. Moreover, critics have not reached any kind of agreement in their assessments of his paintings, as is indicated by the plethora of names that are cited as having influenced the artist: Michelangelo and Jordaens, Rubens and Rembrandt, Goya and Caravaggio, the 17th-century painters in general. There is also a great deal of uncertainty about the chronology of his paintings.

In general one can say that, while a few may have been done earlier or later, Daumier executed most of them between 1850 and 1860.

The painting reproduced here is among Daumier's most significant and one of the most "pictorial." Despite the strong links with his graphic style (for instance, the strong contrasts of lights and darks), the sharp flashes of light make color the primary element of the composition. The scene is marvelously composed and integrated, and the beautifully drawn figures are wonderfully counterposed and related.

EDOUARD MANET
Paris 1832 — Paris 1883
Gare Saint-Lazare (1873)
Oil on canvas; 36 3/4" × 45 1/8".
Signed and dated at lower right.
Gift of Horace Havemeyer in memory of his
mother Louisine W. Havemeyer, 1956.

EDOUARD MANET.   *Gare Saint-Lazare*

The violent reception accorded this extraordinary masterpiece when it was first shown in Paris at the Salon of 1874 was not very different from that given to Manet's other works, despite the fact that the attacks by the official critics were answered by a few who defended Manet, his honesty and his position as the leader of the Impressionist movement. Castagnary, champion of Realism, added his praise, finding the picture "full of light" and "elevated in tone." It is certain, however, that none of Manet's contemporaries fully appreciated the degree to which this painting is truly exceptional, so much so that today it seems to our eyes among the most authentic innovations of the 19th century. To dwell on its vivacity, its freshness as a document of daily life, its profound yet immediate "truth," may seem inappropriate or irrelevant in face of its brilliance as a composition. The indisputable "truth" of the picture comes directly from the way in which Manet envisioned and constructed the scene with brushwork and color, so frank as to be scandalously imperfect, if not even mad, to his contemporaries' eyes. The picture is dominated by the heavy iron railing crossing the entire field of the composition on a slight diagonal, black against the ephemeral billowing smoke of a hidden train whose concealed passing is intently watched by the small girl occupying the entire center foreground. The way the image is abruptly cut on all four sides is one of the most personal of Manet's always unconventional devices. The eye is first struck by the over-all splendor of the picture and then moves to the left towards the beautiful seated figure marking a place in her open book with a finger and gazing at the spectator with a quizzical expression typical of Manet's women.

81

AUGUSTE RENOIR
Limoges 1841 — Cannes 1919
A Girl with a Watering Can (1876)
Oil on canvas; 39 1/2" × 28 3/4".
Signed and dated at lower right.
Chester Dale Collection, 1962.

AUGUSTE RENOIR. *A Girl with a Watering Can*

This exquisite painting is modest, in its limited intent and effect as much as in the simplicity of the setting and composition, in comparison with such works as Renoir's *Moulin de la Galette* of the same year, quite properly one of the artist's most famous works. In the 1870s, which we might call the last years of his artistic youth, Renoir was pouring out a torrential creative vitality that only seemed to increase with age. This golden-haired little girl in a lacy dress stands on a garden path between lawns dotted with flowers and evokes that enchantment Renoir brought to his paintings of children,

AUGUSTE RENOIR
Bather Arranging Her Hair (1893)
Oil on canvas; 36 3/8" × 29 1/8".
Signed at lower right.
Chester Dale Collection, 1962.

particularly in this period. The picture projects a surge of uncontainable happiness. Light bathes the colors, running across the planes as if filtered through an impalpable haze. The child's face seems to shimmer with soft color and glow against the dark ground.

AUGUSTE RENOIR. *Bather Arranging Her Hair*   *p. 83*
Renoir's late years were among his most productive. Impressionism had long since passed, and the involuted classical phase the artist passed through in the 1880s had ended, too, frustratingly, but full of valuable experience. The mortifications and trials of those years had shown Renoir that Impressionism itself had become sterile, but it could open a way to a new type of colorist explosion. The nude became more than ever the center of his attention. Backgrounds were reduced in order to lend even greater emphasis to the overflowing magnificence of the female form. Shapes were immersed in his usual restrained, diffuse luminosity, delicately underlining the way they emerged to dominate an increasingly abstract picture space. It is difficult to imagine a more unified vision; such was the homogeneity of the conception that it seemed capable of penetrating any scene or subject. Only a very few artists in history have been able to achieve a similar vitality of expression in their last years.

EDGAR DEGAS. *Mlle. Malo*
Degas' several portraits of Mlle. Malo, perhaps a ballerina at the Opéra, seem to express his contempt for the merely "beautiful" and to embody his inclination towards the "sensitive" and "fantastic." Even if this work from about the middle of his career is not one of his major pieces, it nevertheless illustrates the essential character of this revolutionary artist who at the very moment of the triumph of his friends the Impressionists pursued with complete independence his own poetic ideals. The modernity of the picture lies not only in its technical innovations, but also in the degree to which Degas impressed upon it his own personality and originality. The little head seems to draw the light upon itself for an instant of prominence, but the light then slips and almost bounces into other key points of the composition, creating a spatial counterpoint, accenting the rhythms of the compo-

EDGAR DEGAS
Paris 1834 — Paris 1917
Mlle. Malo (circa 1877)
Oil on canvas; 31 7/8" × 25 5/8".
Chester Dale Collection, 1962.

sition's balance and picking out certain passages of the figure's silhouette. Delicate flowers, perhaps inspired by an Oriental screen, dot the background so discreetly that the spectator's gaze is focused entirely on the head of Mlle. Malo, noble in the detachment of her intent gaze towards something unseen, unsettling in the subtlety of her features and profile.

EDGAR DEGAS. *Ballet Scene*

In ballet scenes and particularly in studies of dancers, Degas found an opportunity to study forms in motion and to discover new and untried insights. It was for the same purpose that he closely observed thoroughbred horse-racing in the years before 1870, mastering the subject in a long series of studies. The remarkable ballet scene reproduced here is symptomatic of this trend in Degas' art and reflects the climax of its development towards a complete freedom. The use of pastel permitted the artist to integrate drawing and color, or more properly allowed him to think in terms of

EDGAR DEGAS
Ballet Scene (circa 1907)
Pastel on cardboard; 30 1/4″ × 43 3/4″.
Chester Dale Collection, 1962.

chromatic structure. He spoke of himself as a "colorist in line." Here he constructs space along the co-ordinates found in the poses of six figures. The off-beat dynamism of the constituent elements and their strong counter-rhythms produced a scene of tremendous vivacity. The cascading wave of color echoes the movement of intersecting forms across the stage.

CLAUDE MONET. *Woman Seated Under the Willows*
This painting offers an insight both into Monet's mature style and into the principles underlying the poetry of the Impressionists, a perjorative label coined some years before this picture was executed by a journalist snidely describing another of Monet's works which was titled *Impression: Sun Rise*. The term was enthusiastically adopted as the official name of a group of artists who rallied together in 1874 to overcome public and critical hostility to their work. Monet, above all, and before his companions, evolved the

CLAUDE MONET
Paris 1840 — Giverny 1926
Woman Seated under the Willows (1880)
Oil on canvas; 31 7/8″ × 23 5/8″.
Signed and dated at lower left.
Chester Dale Collection, 1962.

revolutionary principles of the movement which was either utterly ignored or misunderstood by most of his contemporaries. Only the passage of time and the verdict of history has justified the Impressionists.

By the time this picture was painted in 1880, Monet's style was fully defined, and it is therefore easy to see here what effects the Impressionists wished to achieve. The transient nature of the world, from which the artist wished to snatch one single instant of absolute reality, is reflected in the rosy atmosphere tinting the sky, trees, houses and the figure which seems to melt into the surrounding landscape. Over the first layers of paint, Monet has laid an infinite number of rapid strokes, each perfectly legible. Their purpose is not simply to define shapes but to capture the resonance of light. It is from pictures like this that Seurat developed the Pointillist technique.

CLAUDE MONET. *Palazzo da Mula, Venice*
In 1908 Monet accepted a friend's invitation to visit Venice, hoping the trip would be fruitful. Although nearly 70, he returned again the next year to paint a series of pictures. These are all dated 1908, but inasmuch as we

CLAUDE MONET
Palazzo da Mula, Venice (1908)
Oil on canvas; 24 1/2″ × 31 7/8″.
Signed and dated at lower left.
Chester Dale Collection, 1962.

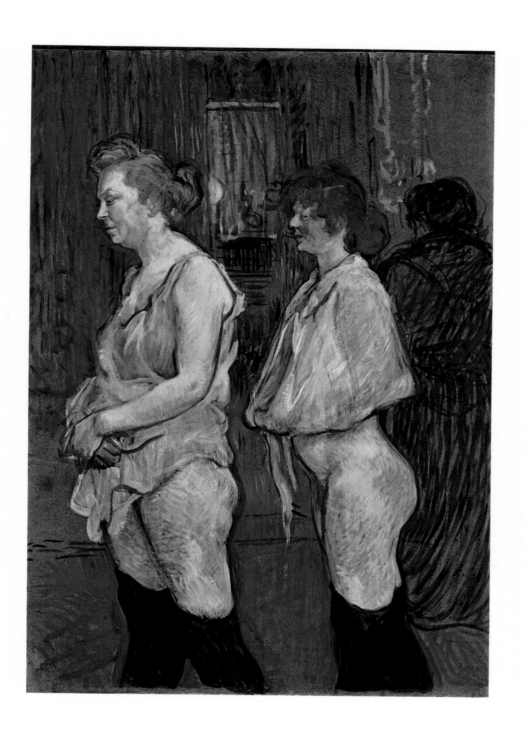

HENRI DE TOULOUSE–LAUTREC
Albi 1864 — Malromé 1901
Rue des Moulins (1894)
Detail.
Cardboard mounted on wood,
32 7/8″ × 24 1/8″.
Initialed at lower right: "HTL."
Chester Dale Collection, 1962.

know the artist reworked the canvases from memory when he returned to France, it is possible that they were not finished until 1912. This picture attests to Monet's utter indifference to the Venetian tradition of pictorial views; it is entirely centered on the play of reflections and transparent light on the water and the façade of the palace. The building itself is simply a curtain of color, situated at an undefined point in space. The Venetian pictures echo the series of *Cathedrals,* painted some years earlier, but above all they anticipate that other celebrated series, the *Nympheas,* which embody the last "impressions" of the already 80-year-old master.

HENRI DE TOULOUSE–LAUTREC. *Rue des Moulins, 1894* *p. 89*

Between 1892 and 1895, in both paintings and drawings, Toulouse-Lautrec copiously documented the life of the Parisian brothels. Shaped by the art of Degas more than by any other influence, Toulouse-Lautrec was *par excellence* a nonconformist and eccentric aristocrat, as is amply evident in this scene taken from life in the best brothel in Paris, on Rue des Moulins, in which the artist lived for a time. His approach to the subject is detached and free of any sensual overtones; in fact, his is a humane attitude shaped by tolerance for the "untouchable." The artist's genius for drawing is readily seen in the rendering of the figures and also in the background where the fleet technique of execution reinforces the immediacy of the scene.

PAUL CÉZANNE. *The Artist's Son, Paul*

This is one of Cézanne's most monumental portraits and close in many ways to the *Self-Portrait with a Palette* of the same period. However, whereas the composition of the *Self-Portrait* is clearly defined and its space given precise definition by the use of such elements as an easel, canvas and palette, the portrait of Paul has no perspective references, or at least extremely abbreviated ones, like the hint of a frame on the right. Thus the figure, with a slight turn to its body, is the dominating element. The themes, or rather the sub-themes, of the figure are repeated in the background, where Cézanne demonstrates his exceptional pictorial sensibility. It would be difficult to find a point of departure in nature for this background, whose function is to underline the solemn yet vivacious rhythms of the forms. It was passages such as this that so influenced Modigliani and Picasso. The paint texture throughout has the lightness and transparency of Cézanne's late period, quite unlike the heavy impastos he favored before 1870. The picture demonstrates Cézanne's individual relationship to his subject, be it portraiture, still-life or landscape. Cézanne always maintained a superb detachment from the incidents of time and narrative in his work, as if his permanent preoccupation, above all else, was to think in terms of eternal form.

PAUL CÉZANNE
Aix-en-Provence 1839 — 1906
The Artist's Son, Paul (1885)
Oil on canvas; 25 3/4" × 21 1/4".
Chester Dale Collection, 1962.

PAUL CÉZANNE. *The Château Noir*

Cézanne frequently returned to this theme, as he often did with congenial subjects, in order to experiment with the various possibilities it presented; sometimes moving close to the scene, at other times keeping at a distance. Here we are immersed in a magnificent, opulent forest. The picture is one of Cézanne's most dramatic, dense works, dense in the way various episodes are articulated and differentiated in a space that expands and con-

PAUL CÉZANNE
Le Château Noir (circa 1904)
Oil on canvas; 29″ × 38″.
Gift of Eugene and Agnes Meyer, 1958.

92

tracts. Within the intricate foliage that covers the land and invades the sky one can read in the lower-left corner a road penetrating a shaded gallery of tree-trunks and branches. These branches both direct the eye towards the descending mass of the composition on the right and link the foreground with the rocky spur on which the castle is built. The composition is balanced on the right by the emphatic lines transvering the sky. In addition to the strong blues, the prevailing colors are the artist's usual muted greenish blues and oranges. The synthesis of structure and color is impeccable, one of Cézanne's most distinctive and noble triumphs of style.

PAUL GAUGUIN.   *Fatata te Miti*   *p. 94*
About 1890, after the failure of his scheme to go to Tonkin, Gauguin still "dreamed of solitude under a tropical sun" (Rewald). His determination was finally rewarded. With the proceeds of an auction sale at the Hôtel Drouot, he left Paris on April 4, 1891, for Tahiti where he passed some of his most impassioned and dramatic years. Masterpieces were produced in this period under impossible conditions of ill health, dire poverty and the hostility of the island's French authorities. The paintings nonetheless burst with vigor. *Fatata te Miti* illustrates Gauguin's innate decorative tendencies. "His art was at the threshold of Art Nouveau" (Marchiori). When confronted with such works as this it is difficult to understand why critics wished to see in Gauguin a barbarian or primitive. On the contrary, he was a master of refinement, as is clearly evident in the assurance of the picture's extraordinary interrupted rhythms at its edges and its effervescent color. There is no doubt that Gauguin was not merely one of the innovators of modern art, but he also is a key to any understanding of much of the art of our own time.

Fatata te Miti

P Gauguin 92

HENRI ROUSSEAU. *The Equatorial Jungle*

This is one of the last pictures inspired by Rousseau's fantasies of exotic
forests and jungles teeming with fierce beasts stalking innocent prey. It is
useless to attempt to identify anything in these leafy thickets with the
plants of the botanists. Like his animals, they are products of Rousseau's
imagination. It is astonishing that this ingenuous and candid artist preserved throughout his entire life in Paris the naïve grace of heart and spirit

PAUL GAUGUIN
Paris 1848
Atuana, Marquesas Islands 1903
Fatata te Miti (*By the Sea*) (1892)
Oil on canvas; 26 3/4″ × 36″.
Signed and dated at lower right.
Chester Dale Collection, 1962.

reflected in his work. Eye-witnesses report that so great was his identification with the world of his fancy, that he would actually be seized with terror at the scenes he was painting.

HENRI ROUSSEAU (Le Douanier)
Laval 1844 — Paris 1910
The Equatorial Jungle (1909)
Oil on canvas; 55 1/4″ × 51″.
Signed and dated at lower right.
Chester Dale Collection, 1962.

HENRI MATISSE. *Still-life: Apples on Pink Tablecloth*   *p. 96*
Although this picture is not the type we usually associate with Matisse, it has nonetheless all the sensibility, taste and color characteristic of his art. Matisse was formed in the French tradition that for nearly a century had followed an anti-academic course and produced thereby every important

development in 19th- and 20th-century painting. Although in this still-life there is a more or less traditional use of perspective and shadow, it exemplifies Matisse's essential predilection for the decorative. In fact the artist defined composition as "the art of combining various elements in a decorative way." The background, for example, becomes an essential element in the picture. No painter knew better than Matisse how to make an arabesque of color and design out of such items of decors as rugs, wall coverings, sumptuous stuffs, fruits and flowers.

HENRI MATISSE
Le Cateau 1869 — Nice 1954
Still-life Apples on Pink Tablecloth
(circa 1922)
Oil on canvas; 23 3/4″ × 28 3/4″.
Signed at lower right.
Chester Dale Collection, 1962.

GERMANY

MASTER OF HEILIGENKREUZ
Austrian or French, between the end of
the 14th and beginning of the 15th century
The Death of St. Clare (1410)
Panel; 26 1/8″ × 21 3/8″.
Part of a diptych along with the *Death of
the Virgin* in the Cleveland Museum since
1937. From a Munich private collection.
Samuel H. Kress Collection, 1952.

MASTER OF HEILIGENKREUZ. *The Death of St. Clare*

The painting was published in 1924 by Buchner with the attribution to the Master of Heiligenkreuz, so called after the north Austrian monastery where the *Annunciation* and *Marriage of St. Catherine* (now in the Kunsthistorisches Museum) Vienna, were originally found.

The extremely small *corpus* of works by this master's hand presents complex problems. Kurth identified him with the Master of the Paramont de Narbonne; Ring, as a member of the studio of the *Grandes Heures de Rohan* miniaturist; others, as a French painter; and finally Baldass, Panofsky, Francis and again Ring, as an itinerant master, perhaps trained in France, but with Austrian and Bohemian connections.

Undoubtedly the facial types and the tooling of the gold ground speak of an artist close to the French miniaturist mentioned (but also influenced by Jacquemart de Hesdin and Pol Limbourg). At the same time the elaborate and precious linearism, as well as the accented cadence of the figures, recall the masters of the *"weicher Stil."*

MATHIS GRÜNEWALD. *The Small Crucifixion*   *p. 100*

The date of this painting is uncertain. Some scholars place it between 1507 and 1508, that is between the Munich *Flagellation of Christ* and the Frankfurt altar; others consider it contemporary to the *Miracle of the Snows* of 1519. The specialists' uncertainty in the chronology of the small œuvre of this artist is understandable when one appreciates the number of non-pictorial factors that have been adduced in reconstructing the career of such a visionary as Grünewald. For instance, does the emphasis upon an "anti-classical" struggle in his work owe more to the raging religious controversies of his time than to some stylistic choice? Any number of factors might contribute to the formation of such a complex personality, but our confusion will certainly not be resolved if we do not take into account such obviously important stylistic points as Grünewald's relationship to Dürer and thus his exposure to a classicizing, Italianate trend. Even in this small panel many stylistic questions are interwoven with the artist's own poetry. The sulphurous metamorphosis of the Isenheim Altar is replaced here by a nocturnal poem in which Christ's enormous arms, spread against the eclipse, reveal to the world the terrible suffering of man.

LUCAS CRANACH THE ELDER. *Portrait of a Woman*   *p. 101*

We know that Cranach the Elder was aided in the execution of his many portraits by numerous assistants. There even have been critics who felt that the suppression of the landscape backgrounds, the linear description of

LUCAS CRANACH THE ELDER
Kronach 1472 — Weimar 1553
Portrait of a Woman (1522)
Panel; 22 3/8″ × 15″.
A pendant to a portrait of a man also in the
National Gallery and dated 1522.
From a Viennese private collection.
Samuel H. Kress Collection, 1959.

MATHIS GRÜNEWALD
Würzburg 1480 — Halle 1528
The Small Crucifixion (1507–1508?)
Panel; 24 1/4″ × 18 1/8″.
Monogrammed. Belonged to the collection
of Hector Maximilian of Bavaria. Believed
lost in a fire. Reappeared in 1922 in the
Schöne collection, Essen. Passed later to the
Koenigs collection, Haarlem.
Samuel H. Kress Collection, 1961.

forms and the broad, simplified use of color were all devices adopted to make the pictures easier to copy! The years between 1520 and 1540 marked the high point in Cranach's portraiture, of which this is a typical example. The flat, acute linear style rejects the classicizing trends seen in Dürer, Holbein the Younger, Pacher, Polack and Reichlich for a rigorous stylization reminiscent of Gothic art. The Humanist of Wittenberg thus abandoned his splendid early descriptive style, and as court painter to the Elector Frederick the Wise devoted himself to the supreme elegance reflected here in the rapid turn of the headdress under which the face glimmers like a white flame.

101

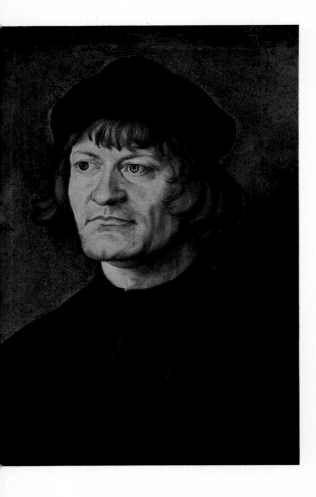

ALBRECHT DÜRER
Nuremberg 1471 — Nuremberg 1528
Portrait of a Clergyman (1516)
Oil on panel transferred to canvas;
16 7/8" × 12 5/8".
Monogrammed and dated. Along with the
portrait of Johan Dorsch, once in the Paul
de Praun collection, Nuremberg.
Czernin collection, Vienna.
Samuel H. Kress Collection, 1952.

ALBRECHT DÜRER
Madonna and Child (1495–1496?)
Panel; 19 3/4" × 15 5/8".
On the verso: *Lot and His Daughters.* On
the left, the arms of Haller von Hallerstein;
crest on the right is unidentified. Formerly
attributed to Bellini. Formerly in the
Thyssen-Bornemisza collection.
Samuel H. Kress Collection, 1952.

ALBRECHT DÜRER. *Portrait of a Clergyman*

Dürer wrote: "When I was young I was mad for variety and novelty; now in my late years I have learned to admire nature's innate self-restraint and to understand that such simplicity is the ultimate goal of art." These words of the old master to his friend Melanchthon describe the course of the artist's mental and stylistic development. The eagerness of the young painter to overcome such problems as the gloominess of his Gothicizing master Wolgemut, or to adapt Italian Renaissance techniques to the constricted space and intense characterization of his own portraiture, is already evident in several of his works of about 1516, of which this picture is one. The influence of Bellini's figure composition and treatment of form and light is also seen in Dürer's youthful style, described by Goethe as that of "an engraver of wooden figures."

ALBRECHT DÜRER. *Madonna and Child*

Of his early works, this is the German master's most obvious homage to Giovanni Bellini. The borrowings are evident in the features and placement of the figures, their relationship to the background and in the progression of the landscape. The Madonna's face is almost lifted from Bellini's *Madonna with St. Catherine and the Magdalen* in the Accademia, Venice. The faun-like face of the Child is a variant on the same picture. But in certain passages, like the landscape and the tassels on the cushion, Michael Wolgemut's recent pupil still shows lingering influences of an apprenticeship as an engraver and graphic artist.

Panofsky dates the painting, with some uncertainty, 1498–1499, the year of Dürer's *Apocalypse with Figures.* However, the vividness of Bellini's influence as well as the painting's stylistic and iconographic links with such works as the *Lamentation of Christ* in Nuremberg suggest a somewhat early dating to 1495–1496, immediately after Dürer's return from his first trip to Venice. Only Dürer's very late *Four Saints* in Nuremberg pays a similar homage to Giovanni Bellini.

PARVVLE PATRISSA, PATRIÆ VIRTVTIS ET HÆRES
ESTO, NIHIL MAIVS MAXIMVS ORBIS HABET.
GNATVM VIX POSSVNT CŒLVM ET NATVRA DEDISSE,
HVIVS QVEM PATRIS, VICTVS HONORET HONOS.
ÆQVATO TANTVM, TANTI TV FACTA PARENTIS,
VOTA HOMINVM, VIX QVO PROGREDIANTVR, HABENT
VINCITO, VICISTI. QVOT REGES PRISCVS ADORAT
ORBIS, NEC TE QVI VINCERE POSSIT, ERIT.

HANS HOLBEIN THE YOUNGER. *Edward VI as a Child*

The prince's small rotund face and his tiny arms and body allowed Holbein to create with the utmost economy an intensely concentrated image. The sharp outlines, the perspective and the impression of mass and rich decorative detailing are wonderfully handled in the rapid ascent from tablet to face, both set absolutely frontally. The prince's gesture, symbolic and at the same time affectionate, adds a touch of humanity to this otherwise luxurious abstraction of a small idol. The handling of the paint is wholly autograph. The subtle refracted light falling from the right wraps around the forms in a way that reflects a study of Leonardo.

This is an emblematic image, abstract and blessing, yet brought alive by the artist's sympathy. Despite the glorious rhetoric on the tablet, the prince's life was brief and unhappy. The picture thus ironically becomes for us a kind of *vanitas* — reminder of death in the midst of life.

HANS HOLBEIN THE YOUNGER
Augsburg 1497 — London 1543
Edward VI as a Child (1538)
Panel; 22 3/8″ × 17 3/8″.
Painted in 1538; preparatory drawing at Windsor Castle. From the English royal and Hannoverian ducal collections.
Andrew Mellon Collection, 1937.

FLANDERS

JAN VAN EYCK. *The Annunciation*

Critics are almost unanimous in dating this work between 1432 and 1436, that is, contemporary to the *Virgin with Canon van der Paele* Altar in Bruges, despite the similarities of the angel and architecture here to the *Madonna of the Church,* usually considered to be one of the earliest of van Eyck's surviving paintings (about 1420).

While this *Annunciation* is not one of his most famous works, it is an excellent example of the artist's genius and the revolution he effected in Flemish painting, even considering the presence of the Master of Flémalle (whose influence on van Eyck's style is often overrated).

The architecture breaks out of the traditional three-dimensional picture space, in order, according to Panofsky's analysis, to make the picture a "fragment of reality." Thus, the spectator becomes a participant in the incorruptible microcosm of the painting. In this humanization lies the superiority of this work to the van der Paele Altar and the reason why van Eyck is more than simply the greatest painter of the Flemish School. His paintings are a world to themselves in which it is easy to lose one's way searching for symbolic meanings; for van Eyck, all life was a mystery and when he found himself before an object, he seemed to discover it for the first time, searching to find the key that would unlock its enigma in order to endow his image of it with a second, silent existence.

PETRUS CHRISTUS. *A Donor and His Wife*   *p. 108*

Although there is no documentary evidence to the effect, it is certainly true that Petrus Christus is the artistic heir of Jan van Eyck. In fact his proximity to the supreme master has often blurred our appreciation of his own individuality.

These portraits, among his best, combine the influence of van Eyck with the effects of the artist's sojourn in Holland. His soft rendering of volumes is combined with a marvelously simplified geometry. His approach to reality lacks van Eyck's sensibility, rather he isolates and describes objects with the curiosity of an alchemist. The artist carefully set the figures before an architectural backdrop rather than against a landscape so that their volumes emerge more strikingly; the heraldic devices on the wall reiterate the emphasis given to the heads. The light falls upon the scene with striking clarity, enhancing the color contrasts and spatial rhythms.

JAN VAN EYCK
(?) 1385–90 — Bruges 1441
The Annunciation (1432–1436)
Oil transferred from wood to canvas,
36 1/2″ × 14 3/8″.
Probably part of a triptych.
Formerly in the Hermitage, Leningrad.
Andrew Mellon Collection, 1937.

Various dates have been proposed. Some assign the picture to the period of the painter's greatest independence, 1446–1449; others shift the dating by a decade to the time when Petrus Christus' style approached that of Rogier van der Weyden, whose influence is difficult to see in these panels.

ROGIER VAN DER WEYDEN. *Portrait of a Lady*
This is undoubtedly the most masterful likeness executed by Rogier, whose powers of portraiture we now rate equal to those of Jan van Eyck. It was

PETRUS CHRISTUS
(?) — (?) 1472–73
A Donor and His Wife (1446–49)
Panel; each 16 1/2″ × 8 1/2″.
Samuel H. Kress Collection, 1961.

ROGIER VAN DER WEYDEN
Tournai 1399 — Brussels 1464
Portrait of a Lady (1455)
Panel; 14 1/2″ × 10 3/4″.
Formerly in the collection of the Gotisches
Haus, Wörlitz. The sitter may be Marie de
Valengin, illegitimate daughter of Philip the
Good, Duke of Burgundy.
Andrew Mellon Collection, 1937.

painted about 1455 after the Italian journey that so affected the artist. The salient characteristics of his portrait style are amply demonstrated in this spare and intensely concentrated composition. The large white triangular coif functions as a background to the exquisite line and modeling of the face. In comparison to another masterpiece, the *Portrait of a Woman* in Berlin, this characterization is an aloof, abstract hyperbole that makes no attempt whatsoever to engage the spectator. The clasped hands are a kind of signature whose starkness is reminiscent more of Germanic Gothic portraiture than of van Eyck's.

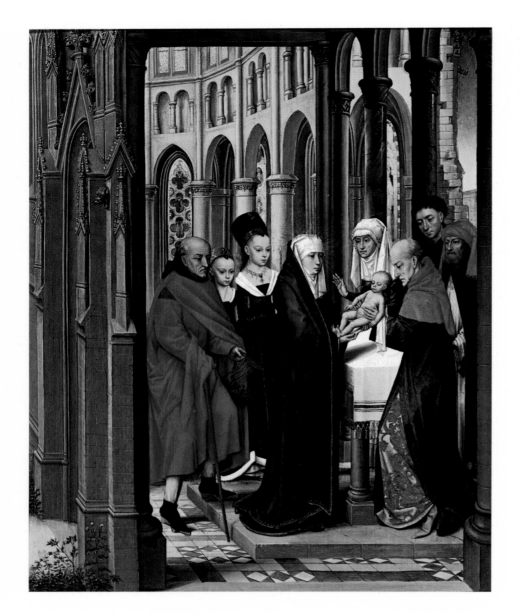

HANS MEMLING
Selingenstadt, 1440 — Bruges 1494
The Presentation in the Temple (circa 1463)
Panel; 23 1/2" × 19".
Formerly in the Czernin collection, Vienna.
Hulin de Loo suggests that this panel, with
an *Adoration* in the Prado and an *Annunciation* on the London art market in 1928, constituted a portable triptych.
Samuel H. Kress Collection, 1961.

HANS MEMLING. *The Presentation in the Temple*

Critics first thought that this painting must have been a collaborative work with, or even a copy after, Rogier van der Weyden. However its many points of iconographic contact with Rogier's *Presentation* in the Munich altar now lead scholars to think it is Memling's work of about 1463, when he was a follower or student of van der Weyden. This places the painting practically in Memling's prehistory, for his first dated work is 1468. Nonetheless the treatment reveals the essential characteristics of the artist's style: absolute immobility of forms and a soft pure luminosity. The emotion thus conveyed is of figures outside time and in perfect harmony with their surroundings. Even the gestures that connect them have been purged of any accidental narrative in this art of extreme refinement.

GERARD DAVID
Oudewater, circa 1460 — Bruges 1523
The Rest on the Flight into Egypt
(circa 1523)
Panel; 17 3/4″ × 17 1/2″.
Formerly in the Pierpont Morgan collection.
Andrew Mellon Collection, 1937.

GERARD DAVID.   *The Rest on the Flight into Egypt*
The painting is dated about 1510, contemporary to the *Mystic Marriage of St. Catherine* in London and the *Virgo inter Virgines* in Rouen, and it exactly reflects David's style at that moment of his career. The way the main figures are isolated in space by the tight folds of drapery is in perfect harmony with the ample background which depicts an exceptionally at-

tractive morning landscape. The colors seem to vibrate in a dewy light that is slightly veiled by clouds. In this setting the biblical scene is treated as an intimate story that has few equals in 15th-century Flemish art.

HIERONYMUS BOSCH. *Death and the Miser*

Death is at the door, but the miser is still undecided between the angel gesturing towards a crucifix and the demon offering a sack of money. At the foot of the bed, a personification of his indecision clutches a rosary with one hand and with the other stores away money in a strong box in which a monster clutches. This is a typical parable of Bosch's allegorical fantasy, but in this panel the interior architecture, so seldom seen in his work, lends the scene a special significance. A receding perspective created by the diminishing horizontals of the balustrade, chest and canopy and reinforced by the design of the vaulted roofing gives the fantastic story a real dimension. Thus the painting is not about dreams and symbols, but about life and human nature, that part of human nature that lies on the other side of reason. The fearsome specters of hell are in the creaking door and inky dark behind the bed, recalling the fears of a child's nighttime imagination.

There is a drawing of the composition in the Cabinet des Dessins in the Louvre, thought by some to be a preparatory sketch for the painting and classed by others as a copy. The direction of the spatial recession towards the right indicates that this panel might have been the left wing of a triptych. The rapid brushwork with which objects are minutely described suggests a date about 1510, contemporary to the Prado triptych and the *Ship of Fools* in the Louvre.

PIETER BRUEGEL THE ELDER. *The Temptation of St. Anthony*

The attribution is much argued. Van Puyvelde, Glück and Friedländer give it to the great Flemish master; de Tolnay, Jedlicka, Genaille and Denis think it by a follower or a youthful work of Pieter's son, Jan. Despite the elevated quality of the work, such doubts can in part be justified. The paint-

ing has strong iconographic and stylistic affinities with Patinir and Cornelius Matsys plus a Bosch-like minuteness difficult to find elsewhere in Pieter Bruegel's autograph works, for instance in the detail in the upper left of the Saint carried aloft on the back of a fish and attacked by demons. But more importantly, the lyric picturesqueness of this splendid landscape deviates from such autograph Bruegel landscapes as *The Gloomy Day* and *The Return of the Herd* both in Vienna and the *Magpie on the Gallows* in Darmstadt.

On the other hand, the extraordinary quality of the picture's execution is difficult to attribute to an anonymous imitator or even to Jan. The world of Pieter Bruegel, either directly or indirectly, is instilled into the painting. The work has therefore been assigned to the master's early years, between 1555 and 1558 and connected with a series of landscapes (*The Martyrdom of St. Catherine* in this same museum, *Landscape with a Hermit* in Indianapolis, the *Destruction of Sodom* in Dortmund, *Landscape with the Calling of the Apostles*), all of which are also problematical attributions.

113

PETER PAUL RUBENS
Sieghen 1577 — Antwerp 1640
Decius Mus Addressing the Legions
(after 1617)
Panel; 31 3/4" × 33 1/4".
Samuel H. Kress Collection, 1957.

PETER PAUL RUBENS. *Decius Mus Addressing the Legions*

This sketch can date no later than 1517, the year in which Rubens devised 10 designs for a tapestry series illustrating the history of the Consul Decius Mus. These were the first years of the artist's maturity, when one can say he had completed, or almost completed, his formative period. Here can be seen the fruits of his careful study of Polidoro, Mantegna and the great Venetians, particularly Titian and Pordenone. In fact, Rubens was more widely conversant and deeply imbued with Italian art than any contemporary Italian painter save, in an entirely different sense, Caravaggio.

A monumental effect is achieved with the simple device of sharply separating the single figure on the left from the varied poses of the right-hand group, which is anchored and given rhythm by the disposition of the standards and banners. In the tissue of color that enhances the equilibrium of the composition, lights change rapidly to darks — darks that are a free interpretation of Titian. At this period Rubens prepared his panels with a white gesso ground that heightened the vivid tonality of his colors. Such panel pictures were usually small, and in a famous letter of 1616 to Sir Dudley Carleton, Rubens wrote, "small compositions come out better on wood than on canvas."

PETER PAUL RUBENS. *Abraham and Melchizedek*   *pp. 116–117*

In all probability this is a sketch or a model for the design of one of the tapestries in the *Triumph of the Eucharist* series ordered from Rubens by the Infanta Isabella for the royal Convent of the Poor Clares in Madrid and woven in 1628 by Juan Raes. The spectacular range of Rubens' inventiveness that was thought to have reached its climax in the series for Marie de' Medici's Luxembourg Palace here reaches new heights.

The composition is a splendid artifice. The story that was to be translated into tapestry is narrated here on an enormous, opulent hanging that a number of putti are unfolding between the columns of a flower-decked edifice. In the right-hand part of the picture, where two men servants carry large amphoras, the "imagined" and the "real" spaces intermingle, the edges of the hanging becoming a luxurious carpet piled up on a ledge. This spatial game makes the right-hand group seem like some splendid bit of a marine

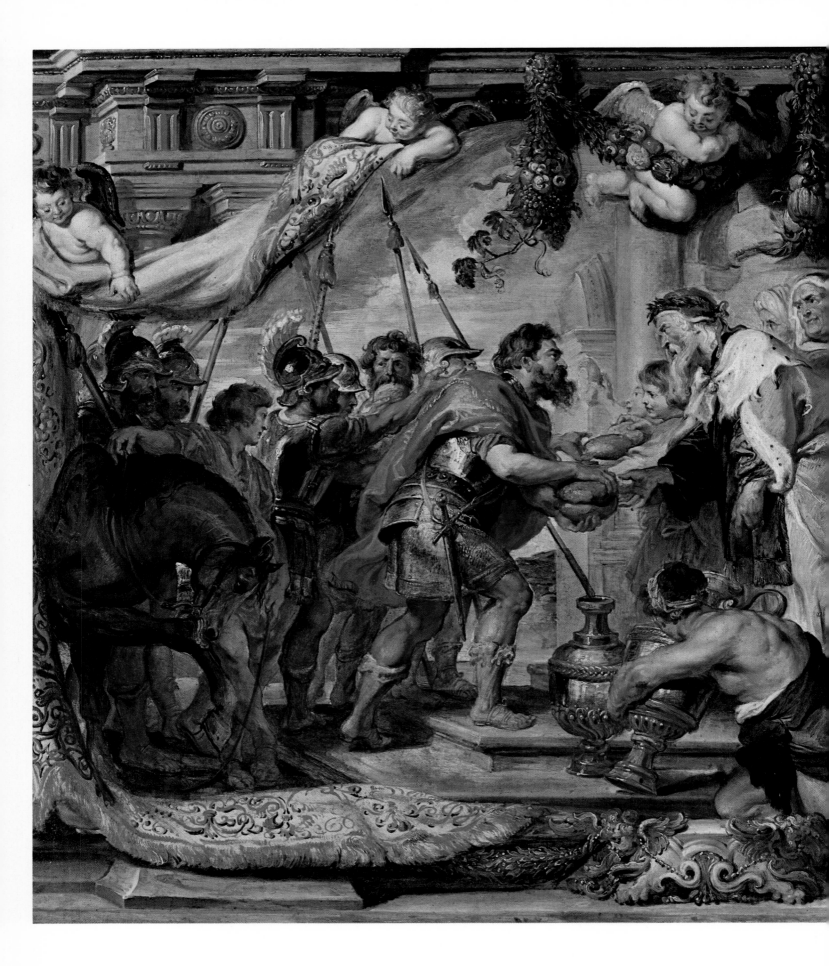

still-life about to tumble from an open net, but for being anchored by the ringed column and clamped into place by the servants in the foreground.

The left-hand group is more solidly placed in an open space with sky, and the figures are set in a tight rhythm of frontal and profile poses. The two halves of the composition are linked with perfect coherence by the poses of the protagonists who lean towards each other like figures in a secular Visitation.

The ability to create such audacious compositions ranks Rubens with Bernini and Borromini as one of the century's masters of space and drama.

PETER PAUL RUBENS
Abraham and Melchizedek (1628?)
Panel; 26" × 32 1/2".
Formerly in the Duke of
Westminster collection, London.
Gift of Syma Busiel, 1958.

On page 118
ANTHONY VAN DYCK
Antwerp 1599 — London 1641
Marchesa Elena Grimaldi (1622–23)
Canvas; 97" × 68"
Widener Collection, 1942.

ANTHONY VAN DYCK. *Marchesa Elena Grimaldi*   *p. 118*
This is one of the portraits of the Genoese nobility painted by van Dyck during his first sojourn in the city in 1622–1623. Together with two full-length portraits of Paola Adorno, this painting is perhaps the most spectacular and important of the Genoese masterpieces whose formal vigor, so firmly interwoven with a completely new courtly elegance, was never surpassed, even in van Dyck's English pictures.

The influence of Rubens, and through him of Venetian 16th-century painting, is here transformed by van Dyck into a thoroughly personal statement far removed from the master's rhetorical and architectonic imagination. In van Dyck's aristocratic vision, Rubens' pulsating colors and hot reflections fade into the opulent monochromes of evening light. In this picture the artist has masterfully compensated for the lack of mass in the upper part of his composition by inserting the red parasol, held by the Negro page at an oblique angle that softens the repeated verticals of the colonnade.

SPAIN

EL GRECO. *Laocoön*

The subject, the only one from the antique in El Greco's œuvre, is from the Roman marble group so admired by 16th-century artists and which El Greco must certainly have seen when he was in Rome. But his interpretation is intentionally anti-classical and unheroic. The elongated, livid nudes in the right foreground add nothing to the history or action; they only create an excited rhythm of luminous zones that is taken up and repeated in the unraveled mass of storm clouds above. Under the dazzling leaden flashes of a menacing sky spreads a stupendous view of Toledo which, in the confusing symbolism of the painting, stands for ancient Troy, towards which trots a horse, pointed in the direction of the recognizable Puerta Bisagra.

The many analyses of this landscape and its lack of relationship to the historical setting of the legend have failed to grasp the artist's idea that, in such a transfigured vision, the view of a city serves just as well as any precise mythography. Surprisingly in such an inventive picture, there are many borrowed motifs. Laocoön's pose is from Michelangelo's *Dawn* in the Medici Chapel; his supine son is from Tintoretto's slave in the *Miracle of St. Mark;* and the Apollo (or Aeneas?) seen from the rear quotes the Escorial *Martyrdom of St. Mauritius* of 1584.

All these, however, are secondary considerations that become submerged in the incredible power of El Greco's style. The light has no source and moves through space like a kind of irrational luminous wind. Objects have no weight and the artist has observed no discernible canon in this proportions or perspective. Such a picture is truly an interior, spiritual sensation. Even the rigid serpents, which have no anatomical conviction or directional value to the composition, point up the artist's state of mind in creating this most unordered, asymmetrical and frozen of his magnificent late works.

EL GRECO
(DOMENIKOS THEOTOKOPOULOS)
Fodele (Crete) 1541 — Toledo 1614
Laocoön (1608)
Canvas; 54 1/8″ × 67 7/8″.
Usually dated between 1610 and 1614, but
more probably executed about 1608.
Samuel H. Kress Collection, 1946.

DIEGO VELÁZQUEZ. *Pope Innocent X* *p. 122*

The picture is one of the surviving 15 variants (including autograph works, replicas, copies and even some signed by others) of the three-quarter length portrait of the Pope in the Doria-Pamphili collection in Rome, painted in

1650 when Velázquez was in Rome to purchase works of art for King Philip IV of Spain. It is known that Velázquez took an autograph replica of bust length back to Spain, but dimensions and provenance make it seem unlikely that it could have been the picture reproduced here. Certain variations, the more severe and closed expression as well as the curious detail that the eyes here are more brownish than the blue of the Doria portrait, suggest that the Washington version may be a first sketch for the official portrait and therefore not only autograph but of great interest as documenting the genesis of a masterpiece. Such a hypothesis is all the more likely when one looks at the pungent intensity of the Pope's gaze and the extraordinary latent vitality of the face, all rendered in the summary yet refined technique typical of Velázquez, here seen at a moment when his style approached once again to that of his ideal, Titian.

DIEGO VELÁZQUEZ
Seville 1599 — Madrid 1660
Pope Innocent X (1650?)
Canvas; 19 1/2″ × 16 1/4″.
Acquired in England for Catherine the Great.
Later in the Hermitage, Leningrad.
Andrew Mellon Collection, 1937.

DIEGO VELÁZQUEZ. *The Needlewoman*

An identification of the sitter as Velázquez' daughter, Francesca, is, to say the least, uncertain. This picture is perhaps the one described in the inventory of the artist's studio as "a head of a woman who is sewing," a curious phrase which can probably be interpreted to mean that just the head was finished while the rest of the composition might have been only sketched

DIEGO VELÁZQUEZ
The Needlewoman (1640?)
Canvas; 29 1/8″ × 23 5/8″.
Andrew Mellon Collection, 1937.

out and left unfinished. Such an interpretation would apply to this picture which is in fact unfinished, intentionally for the sake of expressiveness as is sometimes the case in the artist's portraits, or unintentionally, we shall never know.

The painting is a precious record of Velázquez' method of painting a picture. The large, simplified zones of color in the lower part of the composition and the explicitly receding diagonals show the beginnings of a concavity out of which the inclined head and already elaborated hair would have shimmered in that trembling atmosphere that already invests the face. Besides its exceptional interest as a demonstration of the artist's working techniques, the painting confirms Velázquez' extraordinary ability to communicate, even in an unfinished work, the power of his poetry.

BARTOLOMÉ ESTEBAN MURILLO. *A Girl and Her Duenna*
A frame within a frame, one of Murillo's favorite devices, shades a luminous and smiling image of a girl and her duenna, half-concealed behind a shawl. The picture demonstrates Murillo's marvelous technical virtuosity. His control of light and atmosphere as it falls tenderly on the girl, the measured rhythms of the composition stepped diagonally towards the left, and the assured choice of subject readily reveal his sympathetic and rich vitality. He achieves his effects so effortlessly and with such brilliant elegance that many have grievously mistaken his reserved, unrhetorical and unheroic mastery for mere sentimentality.

FRANCISCO DE GOYA. *The Marquesa de Pontejos*   *p. 126*
Doña Maria Antonia Moninos, Marquesa de Pontejos, was portrayed by Goya in 1787. Perhaps the most singular feature of this remarkable picture is the almost infantile proliferation of ornament — lace and flowers, ribbons and veils, stuffs and bows — scattered so gracefully over this thin, compact, tiny figure. Yet the mechanical and angular pose keeps her suspended in a precarious equilibrium that is halfway between detached dignity and overelaborate haughtiness.

Goya has placed this disconcerting, fragile figure before a schematic landscape that does not describe space as much as it provides a foil to the flood of precious color sprinkled over the figure. The ample sky seems to shimmer with tones of mother-of-pearl that are reflected in the silvered luminosity of the smoky hues of the dress.

BARTOLOMÉ ESTEBAN MURILLO
Seville 1617 — Seville 1682
A Girl and Her Duenna (1670?)
Canvas; 50 1/4″ × 41 3/4″.
Acquired from the Duke of Almadóvar by the British ambassador Lord Heytesbury.
Widener Collection, 1942.

FRANCISCO DE GOYA
Fuentedotodos 1746 — Bordeaux 1828
The Marquesa de Pontejos (1787)
Canvas; 83″ × 49 3/4″.
Formerly in the collection of the
Marqués de Miraflores y de Pontejos.
Andrew Mellon Collection, 1937.

FRANCISCO DE GOYA
Don Bartolomé Sureda (1805)
Canvas; 47 1/8" × 31 1/4".
Gift of Mr. and Mrs. P. H. B. Frelinghuysen
in memory of her father and mother, Mr.
and Mrs. H. O. Havemeyer, 1941.

FRANCISCO DE GOYA.   *Don Bartolomé Sureda*

Sureda, director of the Buen Retiro porcelain factory, and his wife, Teresa, were portrayed by Goya in that active and happy period between 1805 and the Restoration, when the artist painted so many of the Madrid bourgeoisie. But here the real protagonist is color: the marvelous grey with veins of silvery and leaden tones, the play of white and scorching red of the flesh and the live and tenacious fire of the hat. The dense color, applied in broad strokes with sudden glittering lights and heavy impastos, becomes a kind of complex and rousing adventure, but controlled and masterfully fused in the hot atmosphere. The young man is leaning against a table in a natural and handsome pose; the play of angular rhythms creates space and movement within the apparent simplicity of the composition.

127

PABLO PICASSO. *Family of Saltimbanques*
The picture dates from Picasso's Rose Period, which in contrast to the
preceding Blue Period, was characterized by a warmer range of colors and
greater objectivity in his narratives. This is one of the most complex of the
works executed in that year, most of which also treat strolling circus
themes. Picasso's enthusiasm for the acrobats was genuine, but he used the
motif as a pretext for depicting human situations wherein the external
world is merely a mask laid over an underlying significance. Here an assort-
ment of estranged, alienated figures with no compositional or emotional
relationship to one another stare downwards to the right, towards some
point outside the picture, a setting, without space and time, for the artist's
refined drawing and treatment of color.

PABLO PICASSO
Málaga 1881 —
Family of Saltimbanques (1905)
Canvas; 83 3/4″ × 90 3/8″.
Chester Dale Collection, 1962.

HOLLAND

LUCAS VAN LEYDEN
Leyden 1494 — Leyden 1533
The Card Players (1508–10?)
Wood; 22 1/8″ × 24″.
Samuel H. Kress Collection, 1961.

LUCAS VAN LEYDEN.   *The Card Players*

A date about 1520 has been proposed for this picture, but its minutely
measured and constructed space as well as the strident relationships within
the limited range of colors suggest that it might be an earlier work of about
1508–1510. The years prior to 1512 were those of the artist's greatest
originality as a painter and engraver, the period of such master prints
works as *The Milkmaid, Ecce Homo* and *The Prodigal Son*. The view that
Lucas van Leyden was a genre painter whose training as an engraver limited the range of his imagination to narrative works of scant formal merit
has hampered attempts properly to reconstruct and evaluate his œuvre. In
this vivacious scene, for instance, the stepped spatial composition, the con-
verging gestures, and the treatment of the setting and objects already anticipate the Dutch 17th-century genre painters.

130

JAN VAN SCOREL
Schoorl 1495 — Utrecht 1562
The Rest on the Flight into Egypt
(circa 1519–1524)
Panel; 22 3/4″ × 29 1/2″.
Samuel H. Kress Collection, 1961.

JAN VAN SCOREL.   *The Rest on the Flight into Egypt*
The painting was probably executed during the artist's first visit to Italy
(1519–1524) or immediately after his return to the Netherlands. It is one
of the most lucid demonstrations of the effect Italian Renaissance art had
upon Dutch painting. The Child is clearly drawn from Michelangelo and
his relationship to the pyramidal mass of the Virgin echoes Andrea del
Sarto's *Charity,* painted for and owned by Francis I of France, but well
known through copies. The same Italianizing influences are apparent in
the relationship of these figures to the landscape, which recalls Venetian
models that the artist might have known either directly or through Dürer's
art. The painting's precious composition and descriptive detail, as well as
its fine proportions, place it in the front rank of Lowland Mannerist works.   **131**

FRANS HALS
Antwerp circa 1581–85 — Haarlem 1666
Portrait of an Officer (1635–48)
Canvas; 33 3/4" × 27".
In 1779, in the Walpole collection,
Norfolk, England.
Andrew Mellon Collection, 1937.

FRANS HALS. *Portrait of an Officer*

This painting is one of Frans Hals's masterpieces, and was probably executed between 1635 and 1648. In contrast to the festively colored works prior to 1630–1635, the pictures of this later period tend to have a harmonious and intense golden tone, sometimes almost monochromatic, that is often thought to reflect the influence of Rembrandt. But apart from their being contemporaries, the two painters were quite different, as is immediately evident in the rapid improvisation of Hals's unpremeditated brushwork. He created his portraits directly on the canvas without preparatory studies. This direct technique that so well captured the psychology and mood of his sitters became his style, canceling out every other influence to which he might have been exposed.

FRANS HALS. *Portrait of an Elderly Woman*

The typical relationship of Hals's color elements is even more evident here than in the *Portrait of an Officer*. Against the two tones of background and

FRANS HALS
Portrait of an Elderly Lady (1633)
Canvas; 40 1/4" × 34". Signed and dated.
It may be a pendant to the *Portrait of an
Old Man* in The Frick Collection, New York.

132

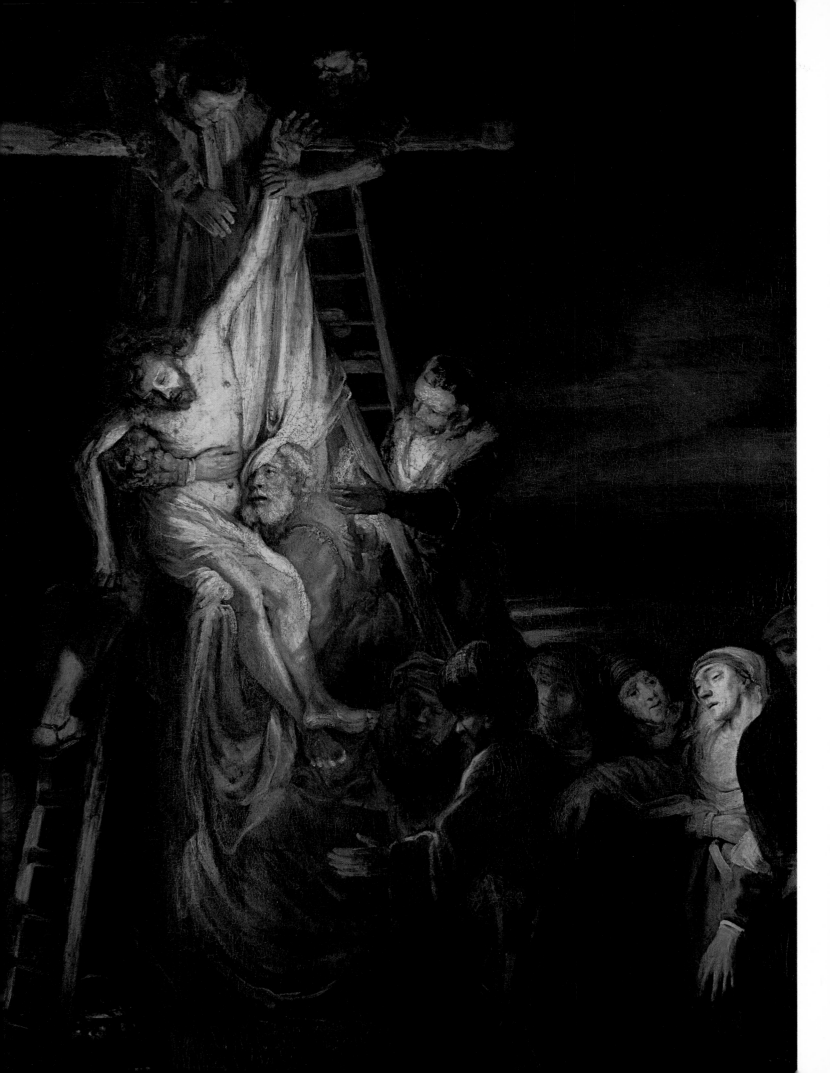

drapery, the sitter's hands and face are juxtaposed with an imperious vivacity. The head, enclosed by the oval coif and set on the large round collar, well embodies the vivid and aggressively sympathetic style of the master. The old lady seems engaged in a lively colloquy with posterity.

REMBRANDT HARMENSZOON
VAN RIJN
Leyden 1606 — Rozengracht 1669
The Descent from the Cross (1653)
Canvas; 56 1/4″ × 43 3/4″.
Signed and dated.
Widener Collection, 1942.

REMBRANDT. *The Descent from the Cross*
This painting of 1653 is closely linked to the earlier 1634 treatment of the theme now in the Hermitage in Leningrad. When returning to the subject after a space of 20 years, Rembrandt adopted the same composition but cut it down with an almost cinematic effect, framing in the immediate foreground only the left zone of the earlier composition containing the two main fulcrums of the drama: the body of Christ and His fainting mother. It is significant that the fourth state of the *Three Crosses* etching in this same year similarly suppressed the symmetry of that composition by eliminating the right-hand cross. So here, the stern right angle formed by the cross and the balustrade of three-quarter length figures eliminates any sense of space and focuses attention on Christ being received into the arms of the grieving Nicodemus. The light bathing the broken body is reflected across the picture to incorporate the Mater Dolorosa in the drama. Such expressive use of space and light was never surpassed in the master's work.

REMBRANDT. *Self-Portrait*   *p. 136*
In his old age, Rembrandt took up the study of his own face once again with renewed concentration. Of the more than 30 securely attributed self-portraits in oil (including those in fancy dress and his self-portrait with Saskia), about two-thirds were done from 1650 onwards. These self-portraits comprise one of the world's greatest diaries, in which Rembrandt's character is tellingly revealed. None are sentimental characterizations. Rembrandt found in his own face a mobile and docile subject, full of luminous emotion and one that he could alter, deform and abstract as he pleased. Sometimes, as in the Cologne *Self-Portrait,* he reduced his face to a sharp almost grotesque mask; at other times, as in the Uffizi *Self-Portrait,*

REMBRANDT HARMENSZOON
VAN RIJN
Self-Portrait (1658–1660)
Canvas; 33 1/4" × 26".
Formerly in the collection of the
Duke of Buccleuch.
Andrew Mellon Collection, 1937.

REMBRANDT HARMENSZOON
VAN RIJN
Portrait of a Lady with an
Ostrich-Feather Fan (circa 1667)
Detail.
Canvas; 39 1/4" × 32 5/8".
Signed and inscribed at left:
"Rembrandt f. 166–(?)."
From the Youssoupoff collection,
St. Petersburg.
Widener Collection, 1942.

he depicts a mood of intense resignation. The Washington portrait speaks of heroic old age. It is one of two self-portraits in the National Gallery, and is universally dated between 1658 and 1660. The intensity of the face beneath the beret is underlined by the cheek pressed against the collar. As in the Vienna *Self-Portrait,* the eyes have a stabbing penetration.

REMBRANDT. *Portrait of a Lady with an Ostrich-Feather Fan*
This and its pendant, *Portrait of a Gentleman with a Tall Hat and Gloves,* in the same collection, are among the greatest of Rembrandt's late portraits.

Light has a particular importance in the equilibrium of this composition, both in defining planes and space and in generating emotion. In the detail reproduced here, the way the face emerges, suspended between the dark of the background and the luminosity of the ample collar, underlines the intensity of the characterization which is not a distracting psychological description but a sensitive inquiry. The internal cadence of the portrait is so profound and compelling that the earrings, pendant and jeweled bow become merely concentrations of light, not autonomous visual episodes.

JAN VERMEER. *The Girl with a Red Hat*   *p. 138*
Given the similarities in size, model, decorative motifs and background, one can consider this a pendant to the *Young Girl with a Flute,* also in Washington. It has been dated about 1665, and despite the doubts of some scholars, indeed a very few, the painting is considered among the best of Vermeer's last period. Such spatial synthesis is found only in the Louvre *Lacemaker* and the Frankfurt *Geographer.* In the foreground the expected perfect description of forms dissolves into globules of light, a vivid reference to Rembrandt's same preoccupation with the essential nature of people and objects, and one that contradicts the simplistic view that Vermeer was only an ecstatic still-life painter utterly immersed in the miracle of his own incorruptible perfection.

JAN VERMEER
Delft 1632 — Delft 1675
The Girl with a Red Hat (circa 1665)
Wood; 9 1/8" × 7 1/8".
Bought at an 1822 Paris auction by Lafontaine. Formerly in the Atthalin collection, Colmar.
Andrew Mellon Collection, 1937.

JAN VERMEER. *A Woman Weighing Gold*

The allegory of the picture turns on the relationship between the woman weighing gold and the Last Judgment depicted in the painting hanging on the wall. The same subject, without the symbolic references, appears in a small painting in Berlin formerly attributed to Vermeer, but now properly recognized to be the work of Pieter de Hooch, about 1664. The composition here was anticipated in the artist's youthful works, such as *The Young Girl and the Soldier,* even to the spatial recession and the setting of the figure, a twin to the Amsterdam *Lady in Blue Reading a Letter* and the Berlin *Woman Looking in a Mirror*. The reflected luminosity is particularly diffused and seems to endow objects with a weightless quality. For this reason, the proportions and perspective, in comparison to Vermeer's earlier works, seem to acquire a greater rhythmic sensibility and poetic power.

JAN VERMEER
A Woman Weighing Gold (1660–65)
Canvas; 16 3/4" × 15".
Formerly in the
Ségur-Perier collection, Paris.
Widener Collection, 1942.

JACOB VAN RUISDAEL. *Forest Scene*

Jacob van Ruisdael is often called the first "modern" landscape painter by those who see in his work the beginnings of a trend that culminated in the Barbizon School. It is certainly true that in comparison to landscapists of an earlier generation, like Molijn, van Goyen and Solomon van Ruysdael, Jacob rose above the academic conventions of his time. But this was owing more to the force of his poetic innovations than to any rejection of traditional models, which in fact often appear completely unchanged in his work. This *Forest Scene* is a typical example of the master's intense lyric vision. The traditional landscape convention has been endowed with a strong rhythmic development of undulating masses and reverberating luminosity. Some have thought this to reflect a pre-Romantic attitude towards nature when in fact it was only building on, and refining of, the landscape tradition which the artist inherited.

JACOB VAN RUISDAEL
Haarlem circa 1628 — Amsterdam (?) 1682
Forest Scene (circa 1660–65)
Canvas; 41 1/2″ × 51 1/2″.
Widener Collection, 1942.

GERARD TER BORCH. *The Suitor's Visit*
Courtly conventions and manners are the central themes of Ter Borch's art.
The grace of the suitor's greeting in the foreground, accented by the little
dog, is echoed in the background by a girl playing a lute. The inconse-
quential narrative is nonetheless rigorously structured by the exact divisions
of space in the foreground and a clearly articulated perspective recession
into the background. The off-centered emphasis on the left-hand portion of
the picture underlines its narrative content. As in de Hooch and Metsu,
light shimmers in the room and around the people in this finely calibrated
human story.

VINCENT VAN GOGH. *La Mousmé*   *p. 142*
In July 1888, van Gogh wrote to Émile Bernard, "I have just now finished
the portrait of a 13-year-old girl with brown eyes, black hair and eyebrows

and yellowish grey skin. The plain background is strongly colored in the manner of Veronese. The girl is dressed in a jacket of blood red and violet stripes and a blue skirt with orange polka dots. In her hand is an oleander flower. I am so exhausted that I cannot even write." The artist also mentioned the picture in a letter to his brother, Theo, including a sketch of it.

The portrait was painted during what was perhaps van Gogh's only stable and happy period, during his stay at Arles in the summer of 1888. At that time he was experimenting with his language of "pure colors" set in pulsatingly sharp contrasts and applied with emotionally charged strokes. The results were exactly opposite to those gloomy meditations and self-doubts that weigh so heavily in much of his earlier work.

VINCENT VAN GOGH
Groot Zundert 1853 — Auvers-sur-Oise 1890
La Mousmé (1888)
Canvas; 26 7/8″ × 23 3/4″.
Collections: J. van Gogh-Bonger, Amsterdam; Carl Sternheim, La Hulpe, Belgium; Alphonse Kann, St. Germain-en-Laye, France; J. B. Stang, Oslo.
Chester Dale Collection, 1962.

ENGLAND

SIR JOSHUA REYNOLDS. *Lady Elizabeth Delmé and Her Children*
Reynolds was so prolific a portraitist that some 2,000 works survive and these vary greatly in conception and style. He once said that, "it is by studying the inventions of others that one learns to invent." In fact his portrait style owes more to his wide-ranging eclecticism than to the real appearances and the personalities of his sitters. For instance, this elegantly refined image of a family of English aristocrats, painted about 1778, is reminiscent of Correggio in the figures and van Dyck in the landscape. These landscapes were a much favored element in English portraiture and

SIR JOSHUA REYNOLDS
Plympton (Plymouth) 1723 — London 1792
*Lady Elizabeth Delmé and
Her Children* (1777–1780)
Canvas; 94″ × 58 1/8″.
In the Delmé family and subsequently in the Wertheimer and Morgan collections.
Andrew Mellon Collection, 1937.

144

reflect the 18th-century picturesque view of nature. A warm light spreads through the two allées in the woods, striking metallically on the tree trunks and illuminating the dense foliage before filtering softly and calmly over the figure group. This "spontaneous synthesis" fully illustrates the exceptional qualities of Reynolds' mastery.

THOMAS GAINSBOROUGH
Sudbury 1727 — London 1788
Master John Heathcote (1770)
Canvas; 50″ × 39 7/8″.
Given in memory of Gov. Alvan T. Fuller
by the Fuller Foundation, 1961.

THOMAS GAINSBOROUGH. *Master John Heathcote*
Gainsborough's work provided an alternative to the elegant nobility of Reynolds' convention and illustrates that strain of Puritan reserve that distin-

JOHN HOPPNER
Whitechapel 1758 — London 1810
The Frankland Sisters (1795)
Canvas; 61″ × 49 1/4″.
Andrew Mellon Collection, 1937.

guished English portraiture from its more frivolous Continental counterparts.

In his long and successful career, this self-taught artist seemed to hark back to only one, distant model, the grand example of van Dyck. Master Heathcote, incongruously seen in a girl's dress, is a direct descendant of van Dyck's English children, as they had been passed on to a younger generation by Sir Peter Lely. This picture was painted in 1770 in the artist's full maturity. In contrast to the "sentimental realism" of Reynolds' landscapes, the background here has a bleak air and a rustic simplicity. This convention, which in the hands of Gainsborough's numerous imitators became a formula, is here rendered with a coloristic transparency and a rapid touch that breathes the artist's characteristic freshness.

146

GEORGE STUBBS
Liverpool 1724 — London 1806
*Colonel Pocklington with
His Sisters* (1769)
Canvas; 39 3/8" × 49 3/4".
Gift of Mrs. Charles S. Carstairs in memory
of her husband Charles Stewart Carstairs,
1949.

JOHN HOPPNER. *The Frankland Sisters*

This portrait of Marianne and Amelia Frankland, painted in 1795, is one of the most successful works from the artist's large œuvre. The conception stems directly from Reynolds, who inspired the artist in his youth, and happily avoids the affectation and sentiment into which Hoppner so easily fell. The two young ladies, whose white dresses take up more than half of the picture, are like two overblown flowers. The triangular wedge of light in the upper left takes up the diagonal recession into space established by the figures.

GEORGE STUBBS. *Colonel Pocklington with His Sisters*

By 1769, the date of this picture, Stubbs was already famous for the *Anatomy of the Horse,* published in 1766, after eight years of preparation. That treatise was devoted to the noble form of the English aristocracy's favorite

beast. Even in this intimate and civilized scene, the horse is the most important and deeply felt element. The simple landscape is based on Wilson's post-Italian models. Beyond the grandiose stage setting formed by the shadowy trees there glows the diffused, golden atmosphere so favored by Stubbs. The features and poses of the figures bespeak their gentility. Their somewhat mannered relationship to one another almost seems to spring from the pages of some dignified yet genial romance of the period.

JOHN CONSTABLE. *Wivenhoe Park, Essex*

Numerous sketches and notations survive from Constable's visit to General Rebow's house, Wivenhoe Park, near Colchester, in July and August of 1816. While there, he wrote his fiancée that he was painting "a landscape of the park . . . with a marvelous woods and a stretch of water."

Constable's prolific drawings provide an extraordinary documentation of his development and it is from this source that we can deduce that precisely in 1816 the artist was paying renewed attention to the Dutch 17th-

JOHN CONSTABLE
East Bergholt 1776 — London 1837
Wivenhoe Park, Essex (1816)
Canvas; 22 1/8" × 39 7/8".
Widener Collection, 1942.

century landscapists, particularly to Ruisdael and Cuyp. However, historical considerations seem in no way to account for this exceptional picture in which each element contributes its own measure of poetry to the incomparable silent reality of the entire composition. The scene is unified by a liquid, golden atmosphere and given rhythm by the long horizontals of the lake's banks. Above, the sky, a fountain of light and life, triumphs. Constable called the sky the "principal instrument for expressing sentiment." Here the sumptuous scurrying clouds crown the serenity of a timeless moment.

JOHN CONSTABLE.   *A View of Salisbury Cathedral*
The artist's long friendship with Archdeacon John Fisher and with his uncle, the Bishop of Salisbury, explains Constable's predilection for this theme that appears so frequently in his paintings, sketches and drawings; seen from every possible point of view and distance; and expressing so many different moods. In some cases the cathedral views were simply repetitions of earlier compositions for the sake of examining the effects of a

JOHN CONSTABLE
A View of Salisbury Cathedral (1825?)
Canvas; 28 3/4″ × 36″.
Andrew Mellon Collection, 1937.

149

different technique or format. The artist's approach to the theme in this instance is among his happiest. A magnificent lawn framed on the left by luxuriant trees rolls out towards the silvery cathedral, seen here, for all its historical connections, simply as a motif in a silent landscape.

Constable's summer or autumn holidays with Fisher, first documented in 1811, certainly had ended in 1829. But the latest known variant on the Salisbury theme is the painting in Lord Ashton's collection and the sketch for the same in the National Gallery, London. The Washington picture must also be late, judging by the firm balance of the composition that contrasts with a diffuse, vibrating color, which once again finds its climax in the sky, a soft mass of moving white, touched with pink and gold and delicate shadows, a festive rivalry flowering in the translucent and infinite blue.

JOSEPH MALLORD WILLIAM TURNER
London 1775 — London 1851
*The Junction of the Thames and
the Medway* (1805)
Canvas; 42 3/4" × 56 1/2".
Widener Collection, 1942.

JOSEPH MALLORD WILLIAM TURNER.   *The Junction of the Thames
and the Medway*

In the Ashmolean Museum of Oxford University there is a smaller version of this picture, a work of about 1805, and considered one of Turner's most typical compositions from the first decade of the century, one of the "prodigious and tormented epics" that emerged from the artist's familiarity with the mountains and the sea.

Using his favored themes, the river Thames and a storm motif, Turner created a drama of men and the elements. However, the narrative here is only a pretext for the artist's real interests, which were essentially formal. The protagonist is the violent composition with its battered horizontals and dark leaden color. These contrast with the luminous light in the distant view of a serene coast and the orange flashes reflected off the sails of the nearby fishing boats. Thus Turner fixed the drama of an instant for eternity.

JOSEPH MALLORD WILLIAM TURNER.   *Keelmen Heaving in Coals
by Moonlight*

In the space of the 30 years that separates this picture of about 1835 from
the preceding one, Turner altered the language of his art without affecting
his profound imagination. In this picture, the stated subject of the title is
relegated to the far right as a secondary and minor episode. This is no different from Turner's earlier pictures; what has been altered is the dramatic
content. The epic qualities of the early works are gone, along with the
weightiness of mass, composition and color. This night scene in which the
full moon is the protagonist, is simply an orchestration of light which moves
through the vast space creating transparent reflections and inky silhouettes
edged in silver. In this magisterial scene, the human activity picked out by
torchlight is like the bustling of ants.

JOSEPH MALLORD WILLIAM TURNER
*Keelmen Heaving in Coals by
Moonlight* (1835)
Canvas; 36 1/4″ × 48 1/4″.
Widener Collection, 1942.

UNITED STATES OF AMERICA

BENJAMIN WEST
Swarthmore (Pennsylvania) 1738 — London
1820
Colonel Guy Johnson (circa 1775)
Oil on canvas; 79 3/4" × 54 1/2".
Executed after Johnson's return to London.
The Indian chief may be his Mohawk secretary, Joseph Brant, known in his own tongue
as Thayendanega. Formerly in the Dina E.
Brown collection, Henfield, England.
Andrew Mellon Collection, 1940.

BENJAMIN WEST. *Colonel Guy Johnson*

West was one of the most famous painters of his time. Among his most admired pictures was *William Penn's Treaty with the Indians* in which the episode from American history is enacted in togas within a Neo-Classical composition. The admiration West and other American artists entertained for Neo-Classicism and for the civic virtues of ancient Rome was linked with the republican aspirations of the emerging American nation. Among the artist's most important portraits is this one of Guy Johnson, English Superintendent of Indian Affairs in the American Colonies. Next to him is the figure of an Indian set in an obscure background, as if to emphasize his remote origins and fantastic character.

JOHN SINGLETON COPLEY. *The Copley Family*

Copley was the most original and vigorous of the American Colonial painters. He was born and grew up in Boston where the rigorous Puritanism of a mercantile society deeply affected the arts. Copley's early portraits, like his *Paul Revere* of 1765, have a solidity that many see as the "American" character of his talent. Before he left permanently for Europe in 1774, his portraits showed a strength and verisimilitude that was unequaled in his long and productive London years. The picture here was painted shortly after his arrival in England. The artist is seen standing in the background on the left, capping a compositional pyramid formed by his seated father-in-law and two of Copley's children. The painting is distinguished for its virtuoso transparency and the opulence of the satins, brocades and other such exquisite details.

JOHN SINGLETON COPLEY
Boston 1737 — London 1815
The Copley Family (circa 1776)
Oil on canvas; 72 1/2" × 90 3/8".
Andrew Mellon Fund, 1961.

155

GILBERT STUART. *Mrs. Richard Yates*

Stuart had his first lessons from an itinerant Scottish painter before he jour-
neyed to London at the age of 14. He studied with Benjamin West for five
years and subsequently became one of London's most fashionable and
sought-after portraitists. His style seems to be a melding of all the most
brilliant qualities of late 18th-century British painting. *Mrs. Richard Yates*
is among his best portraits and dates from his mature and best period. The
figure, isolated against a neutral and impersonal background, shrewdly
assesses the spectator.

JAMES Mc NEILL WHISTLER. *The White Girl*

After Benjamin West, Whistler was the most influential of the American
expatriate artists in Europe. This picture from his Paris years was exhibited
in the Salon des Refusés in 1863 and reflects his interest during that time
in the portrait tradition of Spain, in the art of Manet and in Japanese prints.
The large zones of simplified color and the masterful handling of the cold
white and silver tones are reminiscent of Velázquez and illustrate Whistler's
exquisite decorative sense that was to flower some years later in pictures
called "Symphonies" and "Arrangements."

156

GILBERT STUART
Narragansett 1755 — Boston 1828
Mrs. Richard Yates (1793)
Oil on canvas; 30 1/4" × 25".
Executed in 1793, the year Stuart
returned to America.
Andrew Mellon Collection, 1940.

JAMES MC NEILL WHISTLER
Lowell (Mass.) 1834 — London 1903
The White Girl (1862)
Oil on canvas; 84 1/2″ × 42 1/2″.
Signed and dated.
Formerly in the
Thomas Whistler collection, Baltimore.
Harris Whittemore Collection, 1943.

WINSLOW HOMER. *Right and Left*

Homer was apprenticed as a lithographer; later he was an illustrator for *Harper's Weekly* magazine, executing drawings in the front lines during the Civil War. He was in Paris for a few months in 1867–1868, but seems to have been more interested in the countryside than in French modern art. In 1883 he went to live at Prout's Neck, Maine, where he refined his art in isolation. His subject matter — almost always the sea contrasted to the life and burdens of man — together with his independent development and love of nature have contributed to his reputation as the most genuinely "American" painter in contrast to such expatriates as Whistler, Sargent and Mary Cassatt, whose arts were shaped and matured in Europe. This hunting scene of two birds shot in flight is typical both of Homer's dramatic sense and of his assured mastery of composition.

MARY CASSATT. *The Boating Party*

A daughter of a Pittsburgh stockbroker, Mary Cassatt lived most of her life in France, which became her spiritual home despite the contacts she always maintained with her native country. Her art grew out of her Parisian contacts with the Impressionists, in whose exhibitions she participated. She was particularly influenced by Degas, her own style is a simplified version of his, and limited herself to a few recurrent themes, especially theater

WINSLOW HOMER
Boston 1836 — Scarboro 1910
Right and Left (1909)
Oil on canvas; 28 1/4″ × 48 3/8″.
Gift of the Avalon Foundation, 1951.

158

MARY CASSATT
Pittsburgh 1845 — Beauvais (France) 1926
The Boating Party (Antibes 1893–1894)
Oil on canvas; 35 1/2″ × 46 1/8″.
Formerly at Durand-Ruel, New York.
Chester Dale Collection, 1962.

scenes and mother and child subjects. Although her work was virtually unknown in America, the advice she gave to certain American collectors led to the early exportation of many masterpieces to the U.S. In this painting the zones of vividly contrasting color give the figures a sharp definition and a two-dimensional effect that recalls Japanese prints and Monet. The vibrating blue of the sea animates and sets off the central group.

THOMAS EAKINS. *The Biglen Brothers Racing*

Eakins' passion for art was animated by an intellectual curiosity reminiscent of Florentine 15th-century masters. He studied under Gérome at the Ecole des Beaux-Arts in Paris and later briefly in Spain where he admired Velázquez and Ribera. His study of anatomy, photographic analysis of animals and men in motion and investigations into mathematics, perspective and the refraction of light lay behind his own art and his teachings in the Pennsylvania Academy. *The Gross Clinic,* 1875, portraying a surgical operation, records his passion for science and is an important document of the late 19th century's optimistic positivism.

In portraits, Eakins achieved striking results particularly when he succeeded in forgetting his scientific bent, which often ensnared his inspiration. From 1871 to 1874 the artist was particularly drawn to the problems of light refraction on water at various times of day. He therefore painted a number of these rowing scenes, which also offered the opportunity to render the body in violent movement.

THOMAS EAKINS
Philadelphia 1844 — Philadelphia 1916
The Biglen Brothers Racing (circa 1873)
Oil on canvas; 24 1/8″ × 36 1/8″.
Formerly in the collections of the artist's widow and the Whitney Museum of American Art.
Gift of Mr. and Mrs. Cornelius Vanderbilt Whitney, 1953.

HISTORY OF THE MUSEUM
AND ITS BUILDING

HISTORY OF THE COLLECTIONS

The other great museums of the world, including the British Museum in London, the Uffizi in Florence and the Louvre in Paris, are fruits of centuries of collecting by specialists and enlightened sovereigns. Their collections therefore are intimately interwoven with the past of their respective countries. The National Gallery of Art in Washington, D.C. has the singular distinction of having been founded only slightly more than 25 years ago and is entirely the product of private collecting in this century. In the final analysis its riches stem from the modern free art market which has tended to direct most of the masterpieces that have come up for sale towards the United States. Although only a few decades ago it was still possible to buy such works as a Duccio or an Andrea del Castagno that one now admires in this museum, such opportunities already are a thing of the past owing to local laws forbidding the export of art.

The National Gallery reflects the modern belief that a museum is an educational as well as an esthetic institution. Its underlying purpose is to present a selection of works from the 13th to the early 20th century of the highest quality. The Gallery was born out of a happy conjunction of private generosity and public support. Its day to day operations and maintenance are paid for by the Federal Government; every work of art is the gift of public-spirited private citizens. The nucleus of the museum consists of the 20th century's greatest private American collections, donated by their former owners so that they might ultimately be put at the disposition of the American public.

A century ago the United States could not boast of a museum that offered more than a handful of European works of art. A National Institute was established in 1840 in which was exhibited a mixed group of historical and scientific objects, but very few paintings and none of any importance. The story of the national collection began with the bequest of half a million dollars to the United States Government by an Englishman, James Smithson. The Smithsonian Institution was established in 1846, but in the following decades the only significant art acquisition was the Marsh print collection.

162 In these years there were proposals to build a vast museum. Franklin

Webster Smith's plans for a complex of museums, built in architectural styles drawn from all the great periods of the past, were typical of the late 19th-century cultural utopianism that produced the great Paris, London and Chicago World Fairs. The idea was to gather an ample collection of copies and casts after the great paintings and sculpture of history. Until the end of the last century a gallery of paintings was considered something not very different from a museum of natural history. The situation had entirely changed by 1937 when construction began on the grandiose building Andrew Mellon donated to the nation, together with his collection, for the founding of a National Gallery of Art. This change in approach can only be understood against the background of the first decades of the present century, when the great collections that ultimately were incorporated in the National Gallery began to be formed.

It was Andrew Mellon, Secretary of the Treasury and later Ambassador to London, who first conceived the idea of a new national museum devoted entirely to exhibiting works of art. He gave the nation not only his incomparable private collection as the core of such a museum, but also the funds to construct a building, with the understanding that the Government would undertake to maintain it. His idea became a reality when the museum opened in 1941.

Andrew Mellon, Irish by descent and born in the great industrial city of Pittsburgh, was, like his father, a banker and a captain of industry. He was interested in collecting from his youth, and like Henry Clay Frick, another important collector and donor of The Frick Collection in New York, often traveled to Europe to buy works of art. His greatest single purchase was the acquisition in the early 1930s of 21 masterpieces from the Hermitage Gallery in Leningrad, including Raphael's *St. George and the Dragon* and *The Alba Madonna* as well as Paolo Veronese's *The Finding of Moses,* Jan van Eyck's *The Annunciation* and Botticelli's *The Adoration of the Magi.* In the last years of his life Mellon continued collecting paintings knowing they would ultimately go to the Gallery founded by his initiative. He did not limit himself to European painting, but sought to acquire American works as well and thus bring about a re-evaluation of the native tradition. To that end he acquired the entire Thomas B. Clarke collection of American portraits, including such works as Gilbert Stuart's *Mrs. Richard Yates*.

Whereas the Andrew Mellon collection represents the interest of one man, another group of pictures enriching the Gallery, the Widener Collection, is the fruit of two generations of buying. It is one of the most spectacular of American collections and when at Lynnewood Hall, the family home, effectively constituted a museum in its own right. It was given to the Gallery along with a distinguished group of decorative arts: bronzes, furniture, tapestries, jewelry and porcelains. The Widener paintings reflect the collectors' interest in the classic moments of European art: the Italian Renaissance, the Dutch 17th century, the English 18th century. The donation therefore enriched the Gallery with a wide variety of works by such figures as Neroccio de' Landi, Andrea del Castagno, Mantegna, Bellini, Titian, El Greco, van Dyck, Rembrandt, Vermeer, Constable.

A third founding collection of the museum was the Samuel H. Kress Collection, distinguished for its representation of painters traditionally less sought after until comparatively recent times. Samuel H. Kress and his brother Rush, who succeeded him as Director of the Kress Foundation, belonged to the next generation after Mellon and Widener. Their collection was largely put together after World War II and was systematic to a degree unknown to Widener or Mellon. At the beginning they concentrated on Italian art, including the 17th- and 18th-century painting, then only beginning to be reassessed by specialists. Thus they were able to acquire many works before they came back into fashion and became the most important collectors in America, if not in the world, in these areas. An arrangement was reached whereby the cream of the collection came to the National Gallery, works of Duccio, Domenico Veneziano, Botticelli, Piero di Cosimo, Ercole Roberti, Bosch, Giorgione, Dosso Dossi, Titian, Lotto, El Greco, Poussin, the Le Nains, Watteau and so on — more than 300 paintings bought in less than 50 years. Regional American museums received works that were not given to the National Gallery.

164   Each of these private collections could be a museum in itself. However,

the National Gallery collection was even further enlarged by the Lessing J. Rosenwald collection of prints gleaned from Europe's best collections, now numbering more than 20,000 items. There followed the remarkable collection of French 19th-century art formed by Chester Dale. The Mellon, Widener, Kress, Rosenwald and Dale collections form the bulk of the holdings of the National Gallery of Art but many, many other private citizens, particularly the daughter of Andrew Mellon, Ailsa Mellon Bruce, continue to add to this illustrious ensemble.

MUSEUM SERVICES

In addition to its function as a repository of art treasures, the National Gallery provides a series of educational services for the local community and the nation as a whole. The Education Department organizes daily tours for school children and adults, arranges lectures, provides information for the public. The Extension Service circulates slide lectures, films and exhibits of reproductions to schools and other interested groups throughout the nation, each year reaching as many people again as come to the Gallery in Washington in person. The Gallery has its own orchestra that gives weekly concerts. In addition there is a restoration laboratory and a separate research project in Pittsburgh devoted to discovering new scientific methods of restoration and conservation.

The Gallery is thus a nationwide cultural institution. Historically it represents the culmination of one of the most fascinating moments in the history of taste and it is now evolving into another equally significant phase of public service.

THE BUILDING

The National Gallery was built according to contemporary standards of museum construction and therefore does not have to cope with limitations imposed upon the old museums of Europe, so often housed in former palaces whose architecture is often inappropriate to the display of their treasures to a large public. One of the fundamental ideas in the design of the Gallery was to give as much room as possible to each painting, so that it is isolated in space and of easy access to the viewer. Also the works of art are maintained under conditions of controlled humidity and temperature. The building, which was designed by John Russell Pope and completed after his death by Eggers & Higgins, uses a classicizing design that harmonizes with the architecture of the Federal city and is vaguely reminiscent of the Neo-Classical American architecture of the beginning of the 19th century. The painting galleries are situated on the main floor and are arranged on the axis of two monumental sculpture halls and two garden courts.

LEGEND

GROUND FLOOR		MAIN FLOOR	
CHINESE PORCELAINS		FRENCH PAINTING	
KRESS BRONZES		ITALIAN PAINTING	
20TH-CENTURY FRENCH PAINTING		DUTCH PAINTING	
TEMPORARY EXHIBITIONS		AMERICAN PAINTING	
MEDIEVAL AND RENAISSANCE DECORATIVE ARTS		ENGLISH PAINTING	
FRENCH 18TH-CENTURY DECORATIVE ARTS		FLEMISH AND GERMAN PAINTING	
GRAPHIC ARTS		SPANISH PAINTING	

GROUND FLOOR

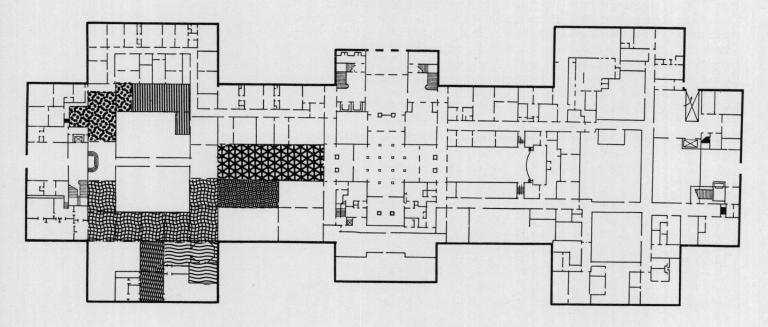

MAIN FLOOR

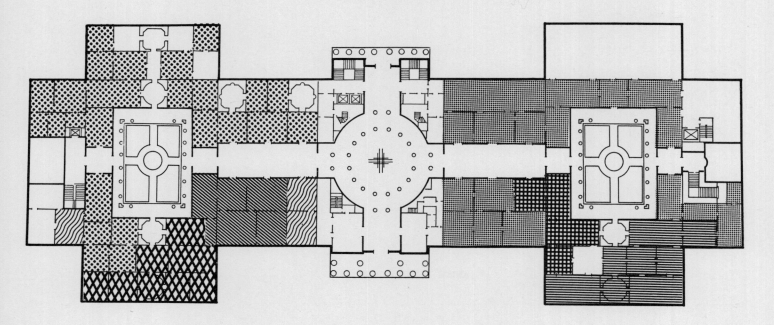

BASIC BIBLIOGRAPHY

National Gallery of Art, Preliminary Catalogue of Paintings and Sculpture. 1941.

National Gallery of Art, Book of Illustrations. 1941.

Masterpieces of Painting from the National Gallery of Art, edited by Huntington Cairns and John Walker. 1944.

Masterpieces of Sculpture from the National Gallery of Art, introduction and catalogue notes by Charles Seymour, Jr. 1949.

Great Paintings from the National Gallery of Art, edited by Huntington Cairns and John Walker. 1957.

FERN RUSK SHAPLEY AND JOHN SHAPLEY, Comparisons in Art: A Companion to the National Gallery of Art. 1957.

JOHN WALKER, National Gallery of Art, Washington, D.C. 1963.

National Gallery of Art, Summary Catalogue of European Paintings and Sculpture. 1965.

A Pageant of Painting from the National Gallery of Art, edited by Huntington Cairns and John Walker. 2 volumes. 1966.

The National Gallery of Art, A Twenty-Five Year Report. 1966.

INDEX OF ILLUSTRATIONS

INDEX OF NAMES

Note: Numbers in italics refer to names mentioned in the captions.

GENERAL INDEX